internet cool guide

SPORTS

internet cool guide .COM

INTERNETMEDIAHOUSE.COM
THE @NETWORK

internet cool guide is an InternetMediaHouse portfolio company.

contents

SPORT

introduction

Attention sports fans: Whether you favor football, snowboarding, yoga, or anything in between, the Internet is your best bet for information on players, teams, tournaments, and more. In the following pages, we've pinpointed nearly 500 awesome sports sites in more than 30 categories, hand-picked for quality, coolness, and overall appeal. With a little guidance from the experts, you'll find out where to chat with Tiger Woods, read coverage of the Super Bowl, or organize a local little league, all online. Also check here for savvy articles on finding live sports coverage, scoring sports memorabilia, and playing fantasy sports on the Net. Looking for a favorite player's site? That's here, too. Not sure what a word means? Check the glossary.

Don't Log on Without it (But if You Do . . .)

That book in your hand? It's online, too. Check out our site, www.internetcoolguide.com, for even more of the best sites out there, plus features, tips, and cool interactive tools. Each week covers a different theme, with an in-depth article, related surfing shortcuts, and our homegrown Top Ten lists. Think of us as an electronic roadmap with the most direct route to your online destination—and a few fun roadside attractions along the way.

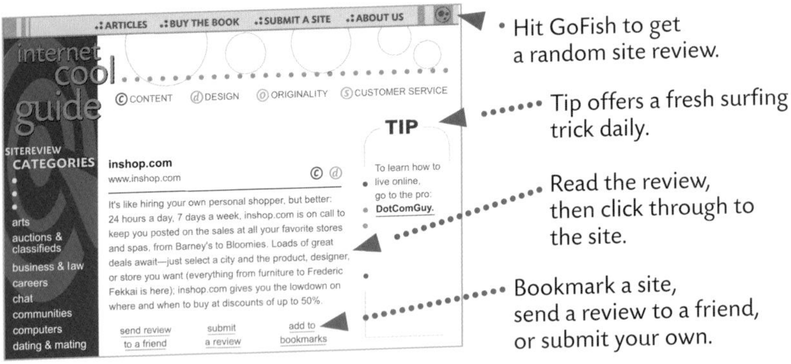

How the Sites are Chosen

internet cool guide editors constantly scour the Web to find the best sites and services around, researching thousands of sites to bring you the small collection here. What do we look for in a Web site? First and foremost, we seek compelling content. Is the information interesting and relevant? Is the design elegant and user-friendly? Do the help pages explain tricky concepts? Is the site fun?

ratings

Rating symbols are assigned to sites that are particularly outstanding in any of four areas: content, design, originality, or customer service.

© content

The content rating indicates that the site offers an awesome amount of top-quality content and tools, such as well-written articles, a stellar list of MP3s, or a big database of movie reviews. Highly interactive sites with loads of personalization and services also get the content rating.

ⓓ design

The design rating is awarded to sites that combine cutting-edge graphics with a user-friendly, well-organized layout. These sites often take advantage of Web technology like streaming audio and video and Flash animation.

ⓞ originality

Sites that receive the originality symbol offer a unique, creative, and sometimes offbeat concept or service. It may be a new concept that is only possible online, or a fresh spin on an old idea.

ⓢ customer service

Sites that receive the customer service icon excel at making the shopping experience smooth and hassle-free. They have detailed help pages and generous return policies, are super responsive to phone calls and questions, and offer a toll-free phone number, a privacy policy, order confirmation, and in some cases, free shipping.

The Wide Web World of Sports

For action-packed coverage of sports as towering as football and obscure as spelunking, there's no doubt that the Net's got game. Here, we round up a few options for keeping up with it all online.

Once upon an October afternoon in 1973, Potter Stewart, Associate Justice of the Supreme Court, was scheduled to hear oral arguments. But this was no ordinary day behind the gavel. Due to a cruel coincidence of fate, the Reds-Mets playoff game was scheduled for the same day. Justice Stewart, who happened to be an avid Cincinnati Reds fan, got through the afternoon by having his clerks slip him play-by-play bulletins of the game throughout the proceedings.

These days, Justice Stewart wouldn't be fooling with scraps of paper, but discreetly downloading real-time updates to his sleek handheld device (tucked neatly in his judicial robe). Although full broadcasting rights for many of the major league events are still carefully protected by the big television networks, the Web delivers a sports experience with which TV cannot compare—capturing events with 24/7 news, endless commentary, perpetually updated stats and scores, and sometimes even footage of the game itself.

First, Hit the Hubs

Say you're a novice to the online sports thing but you've got a laptop, a phone jack, and serious need to see the Stanley Cup—now—and there's no TV in sight. What to do? Head to the big sports hubs. Comprehensive sites like ESPN.com and CBS SportsLine don't broadcast the action, but they do provide up-to-the-minute news, stats, scoreboards, and player profiles. Or check out the NHL's Web site—usually league sites such as NBA.com or NFL.com will have updated news and gamecasts (more on that later).

If you're looking for live game coverage of any kind, visit Yack.com (www.yack.com), an "Internet program guide" that can steer you to online events major and minor—including the Tour de France, cricket, and surfing. If you happen to find an upcoming event you don't want to forget, a click or two adds the event to your calendar, emails a notice to a friend, or arranges an email reminder for you.

If you're looking for coverage of international sports, you can catch a rugby radio broadcast at BBC Sport (news.bbc.co.uk/sport) or head to LiveSport.com (www.livesport.com) to check in on everything from volleyball to horse racing. Both of these sites offer some sort of multimedia feature, whether it's audio player interviews, radio coverage, or video highlights. If you only have time for the score, the U.K.'s Sports.com (www.sports.com) keeps up with the numbers for you in French, Italian, German, or Spanish, but so far lacks in-depth multimedia coverage.

Radio Free Internet

Any game on the radio just about anywhere in the U.S. can be heard online. It's just a matter of lifting the listings from the right Web sites. RealNetwork's Daily Beat (www.realguide.com/sports) rounds up the day's live events, listing radio broadcasts including and beyond typical American sports (everything from *Tar Heel Sports* to *Hello Singapore! 96.3*). Broadcast.com (www.broadcast.com/sports) is an excellent resource for finding live radio broadcasts of everything from minor league baseball to horse racing and rodeo. If there are no events being radioed live, Broadcast.com provides a list of recent audio and video clips. BroadcastAmerica.com (www.broadcastsports.com) is devoted exclusively to live sports radio and streaming news, perfect if all you want to do is listen in.

Live Action . . . Sort of

Not to be confused with the webcast, which is actual streaming video footage, game simulations use graphics and animation to depict event action. TotalSports.com calls it a "totalcast," and at ESPN.com and MajorLeagueBaseball.com it's a "gamecast." Call it what you will, here's the gist: during the game, diagrams map out the action and are coupled with teletype-style play-by-play commentary, so that you know exactly what's happening when it's happening.

While these live virtual games are different for every sport, baseball, with its simple, paced play-by-play action and devotion to statistics, may be among the most adaptable. The ESPN.com (www.espn.com) version displays a simple diagram of the baseball diamond, which changes to show which bases the runners are on during play, while the detailed text occupying the other half of the screen provides much-needed context. Either take this simple approach or visit the

GameTracker at FOXSports (www.foxsports.com). Watch the animated field from blimp view (overhead) or from the pitcher's perspective (facing the batter). When the ball is in play, you can see it on the screen, along with the tiny players running to and fro. If you missed the last animated play, just click Replay. You can watch up to four games like this at once at FoxSports, with no additional mouse-clicking.

For tennis followers, Wimbledon.com (www.wimbledon.com) features its own brand of multimedia experience during the tournament, including a live scoreboard, a virtual tour of the grounds, streaming interviews, classic match footage, webcams, live radio, and the ability to download news and scores to wireless devices.

In addition to being able to follow each play as it happens, an incredible amount of tailored information is at your fingertips at these gamecast providers, such as the team vs. team history, current batter vs. pitcher history (again, baseball), and thorough player profiles. Just logged on in the second inning and the score is already 5-0? In a click or two you can read about how things went down, pitch by pitch, in the first—a convenience that TV cannot provide. Final perk: game simulations provide the easiest, most discreet way to follow the game while at work.

Keeping Score the New-Fashioned Way

When it comes to scorekeeping, "old" media cannot compete with the Web in terms of real-time coverage. All the major sports hubs and league sites offer updates, results, and scores in a swift and seemingly effortless fashion. While pretty much every sports site offers scoreboards or leaderboards, downloadable sports tickers are a hands-off way to keep up with the action. Try the SportsTicker from ESPN (www.sportsticker.com) to stay abreast of scores and stats; or download My Sports Ticker (www.mysportsticker.com) to your desktop. You're on the go during the World Cup? Plenty of major sports sites, like TotalSports.net (www.totalsports.net), make it easy to access breaking news and live scores via cell phone. On the flip side, it's nice to know you can revert back to a less techie time by printing out a blank scorecard and roster at MajorLeagueBaseball.com and keeping track yourself.

Extreme Video

Network television has never had much room for sports beyond the mainstream, and that's turned out to be a plus for the Internet. Because no chokehold on broadcast rights for alternative and extreme sports exists, these events can be broadcast live, in uninhibited real-time webcasts that make the animations at major league sites look quaint.

Networks like Quokka Sports (www.quokka.com) and Bluetorch (www.bluetorch.com) were created to broadcast sports on the Web and it shows. At Quokka.com spectators can experience the hockey game from the helmet cam of a player or see the world go by from the passenger's seat of a racing stock car. A must-see site within the Quokka Network is MountainZone.com (www.mountainzone.com), where you can follow climbers up the mountain through audio reports, live video updates, and dispatches from the trek. As for the folks at Bluetorch, when it comes to surfing, they're in charge. We caught live webcast coverage of the U.S. Open of Surfing and there's plenty more live audio and video to be had in the way of other board sports, BMX, and Motor Cross. Ironmanlive.com (www.ironmanlive.com) also delivers streaming audio and video from the course, with still photography and finish-line videos of each competitor.

And did someone say "wild bikini downhill slalom contest"? Well, probably not until now. Hitplay.com (www.hitplay.com) is an adrenaline-rich video portal that leaves typical sports to the major leagues and instead features an Action Sports channel. Here you'll find clips of a more adventurous nature, showcasing sports like hang gliding, wrestling, BMX, motor sports, skateboarding, and surfing. Of unique interest were the World Acrobatic Hang Gliding Championship, snowboarding with parasails, skydiving with cars, and oh yes, bikini-clad skiers.

Highlights On Demand

Can't wait until the next Tennis Open to get your Andre Agassi fix? Get your bandwidth on and download audio and video highlights of last year's match. With the help of plug-ins like Shockwave, RealPlayer, Windows Media Player, and QuickTime, you can download clips of classic and recent games and play them on your computer. Multimedia search engines like StreamSearch.com (www.streamsearch.com/sports) and Streambox.com (www.streambox.com) are the best places to find these files outside of the major hubs. With StreamSearch.com, you can select and save your own streaming video channels (choose from baseball, football, or extreme sports) and clips of favorite sports load up each time you log on. We found that StreamSearch.com was better at finding specific files, such as footage from the 1999 NLCS (Streambox returned no hits), but the historic clips at Streambox are not to be missed—and you can email them to friends.

Virtually Unbeatable: Online Fantasy Sports

The bases are loaded, Mark McGwire's at bat, and your team's short two points near the end of the season. McGwire puts bat to ball and it looks ... like ... money. The vital question: which team is he on anyway, yours or theirs?

A fantasy sports site ran an ad recently inviting you to "succumb to the sucking vortex" of fantasy sports. To the uninitiated, "sucking vortex" may sound like a bad thing. But if working on that cure for cancer or great American novel is making your eyes hurt, put down your beaker or quill for a spell and try an online fantasy sports league, where gamers draft imaginary teams of real-life players (think Sammy Sosa, Jeff Bagwell) and compete for cash and prizes. When your players score in the real world, you get points in the virtual one. Ask not for whom Mark McGwire homers—he homers for thee.

Fantasy sports first crawled from the primordial ooze in 1980, at a Manhattan restaurant called La Rotisserie Francaise, where Dan Okrent and some of his friends formed the first fantasy sports league—offline, mind you—the Rotisserie League Baseball Association (RLBA). The hobby caught on quickly but was unpleasantly labor-intensive. You chose your players, and then meticulously recorded their statistics throughout the season, thumbing through papers, squinting at tiny numbers, and scribbling in a ledger like a Franciscan monk.

Then the personal computer came along and took care of most of the grunt work. Soon the computer begat the Internet, which opened vast, new universes of fantasy sporting, driving fantasy game players even further away from sunlight and human discourse. Want to get in on this action? Our tips can get you started.

How much is that goalie in the window?

Some of the fantasy sports sites out there charge for membership, although membership does have its privileges—in the form of prizes and hefty cash winnings. The most popular—though not necessarily the best—for-pay fantasy sports site is CDMSports.com, with thousands of people a year signing up for fantasy baseball, football, hockey, basketball, and golf. It usually charges about $30 for entry and small fees to buy players during a season, but the site offers big payoffs—the grand prizes for the games range from $5,000 to $25,000. Two other advantages of CDMSports' games is that they are simple enough for the casual player to understand and you can sign up any player you want, as long as you meet a prescribed "salary cap" (each player has a fake dollar value attached to him). That way, everybody gets to have Pedro Martinez pitching or Shaquille O'Neal dunking for his or her team. Of course, this makes the competition a little stiffer; you have to assemble the perfect combination of great players to beat the thousands aligned against you.

Another engaging for-pay site is Commissioner.com, part of CBS SportsLine. It offers imaginative prizes–win their auto racing game, for example, and get a trip to stock car driver's school. The site lets you create your own leagues and offers nifty software that customizes your league and team reports. Also look here for a real-time player draft, a choice of traditional, point-based play or head-to-head competition, and plenty of free athlete statistics, rankings, and news.

For baseball history buffs, the Diamond Legends game at STATS.com (also available at FOXSports.com) is a pricey delight. For about $50, you can pull players from any baseball era to put together the ultimate fantasy team and compete in 162 computer-simulated games. You can even pick any ballpark in history as your home field. But make sure you have a lot of spare time before you spend the $50; it's a time-consuming game, requiring research on hundreds of past players (usually people you've never heard of) to fit together a functioning club.

B-ball, Pro Bono

Don't want to spend money on fantasy gaming? Don't sweat it. Free sites like Sandbox.com are more attractive to people with just a little fantasy experience. Claiming three million members, this site offers distractions aplenty, including interactive casino and arcade games, trivia games, and lottery-style games for "Sand Dollars," redeemable for prizes. More importantly, it has some of the best free fantasy sports on the Web. While CDMSports' massive leagues can make you feel like a number, Sandbox.com puts you in small, intimate leagues where you can communicate with your competition. Sandbox.com also simulates realism with a draft at the beginning of the season, which keeps the participants from sharing players and makes them work a little harder—since not everybody can get A-list players, some will have to figure out ways to win with lesser-known talent. Sandbox also gives you the option of playing traditional, point-based games or head-to-head games. You're not going to win $25,000 in a Sandbox game, but most people don't play fantasy sports for money or prizes anyway. They play for the glory.

As if to emphasize this point, Sandbox also offers financial games, where you play the stock market with Sand Dollars. If you want to completely smudge the line between fantasy and reality, you can build a fantasy portfolio at Sandbox's auxiliary WallStreetSports.com, where athletes from different sports are traded like stocks, complete with ticker symbols and 52-week highs and lows. Rookie players are called "IPOs." Entire teams are called "mutual funds." New economy, indeed.

SmallWorld.com also combines the traditional, point-based fantasy game with a stock-market game—the players on your roster increase and decrease in value based on their performance during the year, allowing you to trade for more expensive players. Claiming more than one million members, this free site also lets you create leagues exclusively for your friends, and it offers "sortable" player statistics, making player research a little easier on the eyes. SmallWorld.com has also teamed up with online talk radio network eYada.com to bring you live fantasy sports radio shows weekly. To listen in on loud and lively commentary on the fantasy sports scene, check the program listings at eYada.com.

PrimeSports.net has its own TV shows airing on Fox, where real athletes and journalists lend an air of legitimacy to the fantasy-sports phenomenon by seriously discussing it on a real television network. The fantasy sports at the site are somewhat mundane, but they offer decent cash prizes—usually $5,000 for first place—which isn't bad, considering you pay nothing to play.

FantasyTeam.com offers fantasy games in soccer, cricket, and college sports, in addition to the standard sports fare. It also keeps you abreast of betting lines, updates weather forecasts for various sporting events, and even keeps track of crimes committed by athletes. And, as if the Internet needed another place to look at half-naked women, FantasyTeam.com also offers Swimsuit-Sports.com, which proffers video clips of women in swimwear discussing sports news. Here, you can also get pictures of bikini-clad babes to trade with your bikini-clad-babe-loving friends.

Auto-racing fans will love vrace.com, another free site, where you create your own racing team, picking real drivers, pit-crew chiefs, car-body types, sponsors, and even team colors. If your racers win prize money in the real races, you get virtual prize money, which you can use to upgrade components of your team.

Vital Stats

When you own a fantasy team, your most vital resource is information. Will your shortstop's hangnail keep him out of the next game, costing you points and giving you gray hair?

To meet this demand, there are about a zillion sites offering player news, stats, and rankings. Many, of course, want you to pay through the nose for the info. FantasyInsights.com, for example, has thrice been named the best fantasy football site on the Internet by the Dick Butkus Football Network. It had better be good, considering they want $115 for their deluxe "Ultimate Fantasy Web Package," which includes a pre-season report, weekly updates, and fancy draft software.

RotoNews.com, on the other hand, offers its information for free. RotoNews covers all the big sports, religiously recording every player's bump, bruise, and night sweat, and a short paragraph of analysis accompanies each update. They have free and fee-based email services, and, if you're stuck in the wilderness and dying to know how your goalie's knee is feeling, RotoNews will send such vital info to your cell phone or pager at a relatively low cost.

A remnant of the old days of fantasy sports is USAStats.com, the official site of the RLBA. It offers online fantasy baseball and basketball games and player statistics and rankings. The site's "matchmaker" service can help you find an opening in a traditional (paper-based) fantasy league. It's a little dry compared to the splashier offerings now on the Web, but this is the fountain from which all fantasy sports flow, so pay your respects.

If none of these sites light your fantasy fire, no worries, there are hundreds more. To help you negotiate the multiverse and find a fantasy home (or homes) is a search engine devoted exclusively to fantasy sports, UsFantasy411.com. An excellent directory of fantasy sports sites is AddictFantasySports.com.

One more thing: if you're not a sports fan, you'll likely have little interest in fantasy sports. If you are a sports fan, then fantasy sports will make you a better one. Statistics of obscure players for whom you wouldn't ordinarily give a tinker's damn become your stock in trade. And though you might disappear into this alternative universe, don't worry—you'll have plenty of company.

7 Steps to Fantasy Sports

If you've got some sports knowledge, a lust for competition, and a love for the game, you fit the profile of a potential fantasy gamer. Here's how to get started playing.

1. **Name your poison.** Baseball, basketball, football, hockey or something else? Pick the sport you know best or enjoy the most. If you've got a lot of time and knowledge, pick 'em all—you don't go outside much anyway, right?

2. **Find your commitment level.** In order to choose the right league, you'll need to decide your potential level of involvement. Are you going to spend five minutes a day on this, or are you going to base your entire sense of self worth on it? Do you want a simple game or something that will require you to hire a statistician? Low-key gamers should sign up on a site that does most of the number crunching for you; while creating a small league with friends is fun, it may require more effort.

3. **Do some home-shopping.** Visit several sites and take tours (if available), or at least read the rules, to find one that suits you best. Go with the recommendations here (see page 47), or check search engines like AddictFantasySports.com or UsFantasy411.com for more options.

4. **Sign up.** Once you find a site, you'll have to register and decide a name for your team, providing personal details and—in some cases—your credit card number. If you do join a league that costs money, be sure that the site offers secure ordering. Look for a lock icon at the bottom of your browser window to be sure a page is secure.

5. Draft your team. Next comes the fun part—putting together a team. Different sites have different ways of assembling fantasy teams. CDMSports.com, for example, assigns an imaginary salary to all players, and you can pick any player you want, as long as you stay within a salary cap. The end result of such a system is that everybody gets to use the same players. Sandbox.com, on the other hand, has a more realistic—but more challenging—system, in which you and the other players in your league have to divvy up the real-life players in a draft.

6. Do your homework. Not sure what players to pick? It just takes a bit of research. Fortunately, information isn't hard to find—every sports site worth its salt has a fantasy sports section with player rankings and analysis, and there are plenty of sites devoted solely to keeping team owners informed.

The challenge is weeding through all the information. When evaluating players for your team, remember that just because a player is good in real life, it doesn't mean he'll be good for your fantasy team. For example, if your fantasy baseball league awards lots of points for home runs and none for defense, a sure-handed shortstop who doesn't hit many homers probably won't do you much good. Before you draft a team, make a list of the available players and rank them according to their fantasy value. That way, when you're drafting, if your favorite player isn't available, you can quickly find the next-best player.

7. Tinker. One thing is guaranteed about fantasy sports: if you're going to win, your lineup at the end of the season won't look much like your lineup at the start of the season. Players get hurt. Often they don't live up to potential. For any number of reasons, you will turn over many of your players, dumping them or trading them with other people in your league throughout the season. Keeping a fantasy team running on all cylinders requires almost daily attention—just remember, it's supposed to be fun.

Sports Memorabilia: The Online Buy and Sell

Buy me some peanuts and Cracker Jacks? How about a $4,500 Babe Ruth-signed baseball mitt instead? But before you fork over your life savings for that must-have mitt or trading card, read over these tips for safe trading.

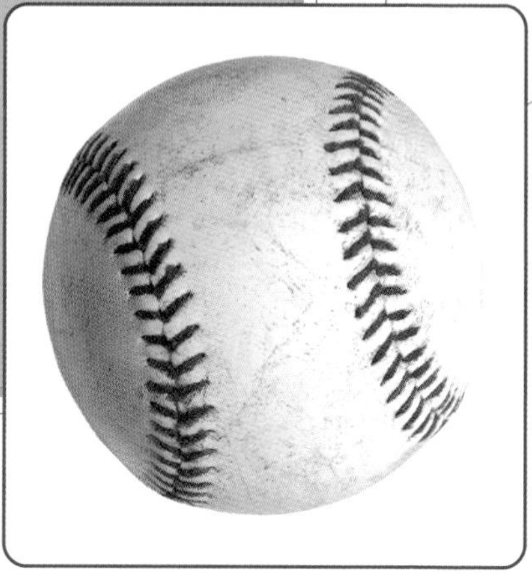

OK, so maybe you don't have a million dollars to spend on the legendary "Mint" T206 Honus Wagner tobacco trading card. Anyone who lives for the swap and quick sell of sports cards and collectibles should check out the offerings online, where you can grade and verify your cards, check their value against an online price guide, or shop for everything from autographed balls to signed U.S. Open flags. But don't say we didn't warn you: false items and forged autographs abound at collecting hubs and auction sites. A little knowledge about authentication services and trustworthy e-tailers will take you a long way.

Trading Cards Grading and Authentication

Grading services exist to ensure fairness and consistency when buying, selling, or trading cards, and give traders an accurate sense of the value of their holdings. The service assigns an overall grade to individual cards based on the condition of several different parts of the card, such as the corners, the edges, and the surface. Professional Sports Authenticator (PSA), the self-proclaimed "largest third-party authentication service," is just what the trainer ordered. The PSA site, www.psacard.com, has instructions on submitting cards and becoming a PSA-authorized dealer, as well as lists of prices of the most popular cards. PSA is the trading card hobby's standard for card authentication, though there are other reliable services (such as beckett.com) to be found online.

Price Guides

beckett.com is a one-stop megasite offering price guides, auctions, a consumer and dealer marketplace, card grading services, and more. A $1.95 per month, per sport subscription fee for the price guides includes online checklists and access to a New Release Pricing Area where you'll find information on cards so new they don't appear in the monthly magazines. My Want List, a wishlist feature for collectors, scours their marketplace of dealer stores nightly. If you have a collection worth showing off, build a Web page on beckett's server to let other collectors know you're out there.

Trading Card Manufacturers

Plenty of top card manufacturers have gone online to offer collectors sneak peeks of upcoming sets or details on special-edition buys. The Upper Deck company (www.upperdeck.com) reels collectors in with a series of absurd card-themed Shockwave games. Join its Collectors Club online, or shop for authenticated memorabilia and collectibles at UpperDeckStore.com. Fleer/Skybox (www.fleerskybox.com) takes its online presence to the next level with a sizzling Flash intro, plus an image gallery of cards, release dates of upcoming series, and a handy search function. Fleer/Skybox's columnists cut through the card industry hype of overrated rookies and new sets, providing an intelligent angle on the sports collectibles community. Card-makers Topps (www.topps.com) and Donruss (www.donruss.com) are also online but offer less content than the others.

Memorabilia

If you're wary of buying stuff like jerseys and signed merchandise from auction sites like eBay, try one of the large online dealer sites, where authenticity is guaranteed. Pro Sports Memorabilia (www.prosportsmemorabilia.com) offers a huge selection of memorabilia items, many of which are autographed. Although the sheer volume (and price) of items on offer can't compare to the deals found at auction, you can rest assured that the stuff you're scoring is the real deal: Pro Sports uses five different authentication services including UDA, Total Sports Concepts, and Mounted Memories. A stop here can land you cool odds and ends like a piece of floor from Larry Bird's Indiana high school, a Rawlings baseball mitt signed by Ken Griffey, Jr., or a Walter Payton-signed box of Wheaties.

Even if you don't have the privilege of attending private Steiner

Sports autograph sessions in their Manhattan headquarters, you can still send in items to be signed by heroes like Mia Hamm and Derek Jeter. Steiner Sports (www.steinersports.com) has one of the most exhaustive memorabilia dealer sites on the Web and prides itself on a vast selection of autographed balls. Rock-solid policies on authenticity and returns let you shop with confidence.

Auctions

At massive auctions like eBay and uBid, you'll find what you're looking for nine times out of 10 no matter how obscure your collecting needs. But watch out for fakes. Just remember: the higher the value, scarcity, or demand for the item, the higher the probability that it's a forgery. (Most of the Ruth, Gehrig, Mantle, and other "rare" and high-demand autographs sold online are fake.) Still, if you're looking to cash in by unloading your most recent acquisitions (or your dusty childhood collection), these are the places to go.

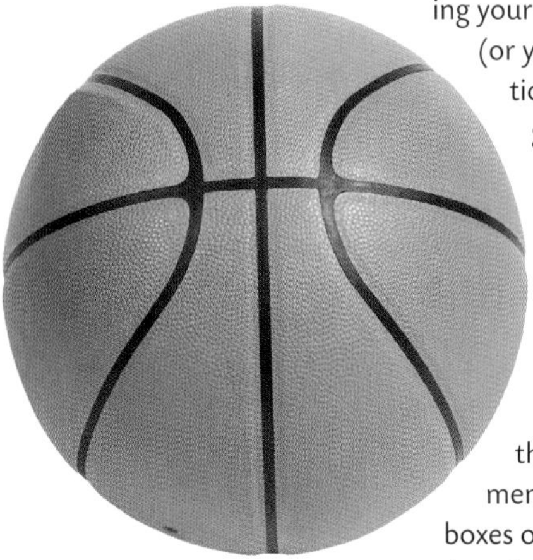

uBid.com
www.ubid.com
Look to the Sports Memorabilia, Trading Cards, and Hobbies & Collectibles subcategories at this auction hub for signed memorabilia and unopened boxes of cards plus hundreds more gotta-have items. And don't hesitate to take advantage of uBid.com's Auction Alert service, which emails updates on newly offered products in the categories you've selected.

Teletrade www.teletrade.com
Offering loads of helpful tools and on-sale goodies for the serious collector, Teletrade remains true to its claim that every auction on its site has a collection of rare cards. Track and Bid lists let you keep an eye on items of interest and set maximum bid prices automatically. If bidding stops before your highest set amount and you're the final bidder, then the lot is yours. Also, the Price Guide search here can show you what specified items have sold for in the past few months—that way, you know what to expect as a buyer or seller.

eBay www.ebay.com

Click on eBay's Sports link to search more than 500,000 listings of autographs, memorabilia, and trading cards for any imaginable sport (even cricket trading cards!). In our search for a Michael Jordan autograph, eBay turned up an impressive 106 results, including signed balls, jerseys, photos, and even shoes. But wise buyers should be wary of the authenticity of goods offered at person-to-person online auctions like these; eBay won't pay you back if the Jordan-signed ball you bid for is fake.

sothebys.amazon.com www.sothebys.amazon.com

If you're serious about sports memorabilia (or scoping for your holiday wishlist), head to Sotheby's, where baseball art, signed photographs, and other collectible rarities usually go for well over $1,000 apiece. Count on finding far more authentic autographs here than on eBay or other person-to-person trading communities. Plus, Amazon hosts the site, so you get a high-quality interface and the expertise of its sports memorabilia specialist.

If you've searched all corners of the online world and still can't find the rare card you seek, you might try a few of the more obscure (but useful) collecting locales. Baseball Planet Sportscards (www.baseballplanet.com) and Sportsauction.com (www.sportsauction.com) provide unique auction lots but work with only a fraction of the volume that league leaders eBay and uBid have to offer. Or click onto CollectingChannel.com (www.collectingchannel.com), which provides loads of news and information for sports collectible hobbyists and just might turn up an item you missed at a bigger site.

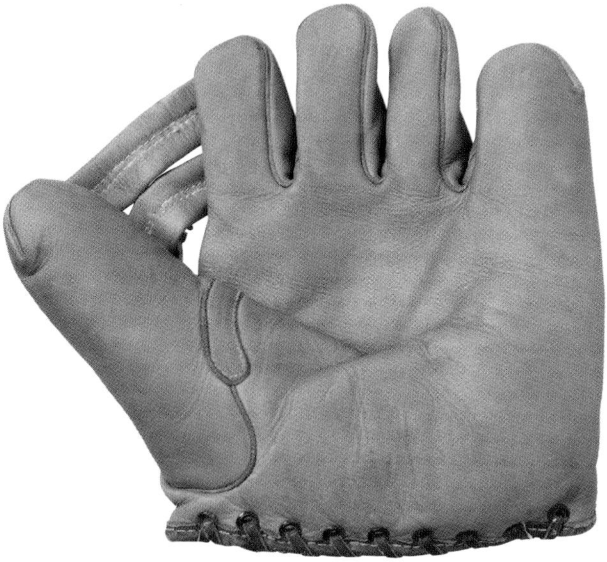

Most Valuable Player Sites

Some would say you're not really a sports fan unless you've memorized every stat, watched last night's play from 12 different angles, and can rattle off your favorite player's breakfast cereal, arrest record, and batting average. But that's just a slice of the kind of fan worship that you thought you could live without—until the Internet came along.

Easy access to the Web has generated a wealth of sports fan sites ranging from multimedia commercial wonders to homegrown shrines of indie commentary and gossip. It's now easy to jump into an international chat on soccer with Alexei Lalas (www.isfa.com), read comics purely dedicated to cycling, or help Miss Anna Kournikova become the most-searched athlete on the Web. While there are plenty of major league-affiliated player's sites that are worth your time, finding those obscure, slightly obsessive, totally fun endeavors takes a whole lot of cyber-schlepping. We map the playing field for you, pointing out the most valuable player sites to shoot for, both major and minor.

League & Network Sites

League sites have a monopoly on player pages: any league whose budget exceeds the gross national product of a small Third World nation will have a great Web site with an abundance of player profiles. If sites like NBA.com, the NFL's Players Network, and NHL.com come to mind, you're on the right track. These sites are the most reliable sources for information on any professional athlete, but all the players receive the same treatment whether or not they're this year's MVP or some benched rookie on the Vancouver Grizzlies.

Sports network sites such as CBS SportsLine power pages devoted to idols like Shaquille O'Neill (www.shaq.com) and Michael Jordan (jordan.sportsline.com), where you can play against His

Airness in a one-on-one match-up, see clips of his glory days, or keep up with his post-NBA putting-green adventures. If high-flying stadium sports aren't your thing, you can also check out sports stars like Andre Agassi (www.andresite.com) or track Tiger Woods (www.tigerwoods.com) as he racks up more grand slam titles and grand slam salaries.

The Rivals.com Network (www.rivals.com) remains unrivaled in terms of sports coverage with its comprehensive written coverage of almost every sport imaginable, from professional and college leagues to extreme board sports and archery, all coupled with streaming videos and audio clips of key plays and interviews. The site, loaded with game coverage, is also jam-packed with pages dedicated to athletic figures. The one drawback? You have to search through the sports or team pages to get to sites devoted to players.

Fanlink Network is rapidly becoming a serious contender, with plans to launch player's pages for 11 different professional sports. Unfortunately, its only functional site at press time, Gridiron.com (www.gridiron.com), was slapped with litigation from professional football leagues. But with any good fortune, the sites will be expanded soon with sports news, schedules, and the official pages of almost 200 players (many of them not-so-major) to which you can email questions, criticisms, or your own brilliant coaching tips.

Until then, college sports fans can click over to Fansonly.com (www.fansonly.com), a network that breaks through all the hype and drama of college athletics, featuring those players that may one day have their names trademarked and domained, such as 1999 #1 NBA draft pick, Elton Brand.

Up Close & Personal

While the network sites keep fans updated on every move in the leagues, devotees who are looking to get up close and personal with their sports deities should look elsewhere for private info, chat, and gossip. Boasting more than 200 official sites as well as news articles, AthletesDirect (www.athletesdirect.com) hosts some of the best-designed sites about players—some with animated intros and all with media highlights and email correspondence. Chat with other women's soccer aficionados about girl goddess Mia Hamm's site (www.miadirect.com); watch a gamecast of the All Star Game on Ken Griffey, Jr.'s page (www.juniordirect.com), or even check out retirees such as Kareem Abdul-Jabar at Legends Direct (www.legendsdirect.com.)

AthleteNow (www.athletenow.com) has a limited listing of athletes but comes with player-written diaries that peek into the quirky activities players partake in after regulation time is over, such as Gary Payton's billiards habit and rap video appearances. Artistically inclined fans can also send in their own rap lyrics and poetry dedicated to their sources of inspiration. One lyrical creation we found on the site was "The Iceman Cometh" by K. Senzapaura, an ode to the Colorado Avalanche's Ray Bourque. An excerpt reads:

I've donned the blades,
Secured the pads,
And chose my secret
weapons.
Fleet of foot with
blinding speed,
I'll come at you
From all directions.

Art, indeed...

Homegrown Fan Sites

When fancy network sites don't exist for a worshipped player—and even if they do—many people hop on the do-it-yourself bandwagon, creating their own fan pages, most of which end up as part of the Angelfire or GeoCities networks. These are often the only sites dedicated to sports figures who don't get massive media attention. In some cases, fan(atic)s will register a domain and create independent sites for their favorite athlete. For amateur endeavors, some of these sites are relatively decent.

The slightly obsessive undertaking anna-fans.com (www.anna-fans.com) is one of thousands of sites devoted to tennis star Anna Kournikova and features news updates, video clips, and original collages called 'LipSticks'—pictures of the clay-court seductress available for your desktop. Of course, you could also go to Kournikova's official site (www.kournikova.com) for some Anna-sanctioned drooling.

Or check out our pick for the best Web site dedicated to über-fighter Muhammad Ali: Definition of Champ (www.definitionofchamp.com). Sophisticated and sleek in design, loaded with history and images, and backed up with audio clips of funky soulful sounds of the era, this site's a great source for information, though fans can't see or hear clips from the history-making fights.

Humor & Spoofs

In addition to all the unconditional online idolatry that goes on, plenty of sports fans have posted humorous and irreverent sites that cover everything from taking cracks at overpaid pro hockey players to extolling the virtues of appliance shooting (we kid you not). A few favorites:

Hofstetter's Jerk of the Week www.jerkoftheweek.com

The good guys always finish last at Hofstetter's hilarious site, where baseball, football, hockey, and basketball stars get lambasted for fights, fouls, arrests, and generally bad behavior. Fans vote for the player they think should get the coveted title each week. Past winners include Ravens runningback Ray Lewis (murder arrest) and former Chiefs runningback Bam Morris (marijuana arrest). The really big winners (losers?) compete for the annual Silver Pig Award or a place in the Jerk Hall of Fame.

Heckle Depot www.heckledepot.com

No one is safe from the wrath of the spectators! This site has different rants appropriate for hecklers in every section of the park—bullpen to field. The site's attacks are aimed at everyone from the batters to the umps and each includes a Top 10 list of players to heckle. Take these to the ballgame:

"Somebody call the law, this guy is impersonating an umpire!"

"Hey Ump, I thought only horses slept standing up!"

Muscleheadz www.muscleheadz.com

Is there really a correlation between brain size and body mass? Pretty unlikely, but John Gleneicki makes great fun pretending that there is. Muscleheadz is Gleneicki's collection of hilarious and addictive cartoons poking fun at muscle-bound jocks. If you like the 'toons, feel free to buy them in all their various incarnations: calendars, training journals, and even apparel.

The NBA's Good, Bad, and Ugly nba-basketball.tripod.com

The title leaves nothing to the imagination—it's one fan's list of who should be hooping, who should be benched, and who should never have his face on a cereal box (lest he frighten the children). A self-professed PG-13 publication by an ardent Orlando Magic fan (no one on their roster is included on the ugly page), the site extols the virtues of the Magic while viciously maligning the "freaking Euros." Don't say we didn't warn you.

Major League Baseball www.majorleaguebaseball.com ©

The only thing missing here is the smell of roasted peanuts, hot dogs, and not-so-cheap beer. It's the official Web site of Major League Baseball—why go anywhere else for stats, schedules, and team info? You can tune in to live press conferences and live game audio from local radio stations broadcasting around the country. There are also video clips that highlight amazing past plays and historical footage from baseball's yesteryear. Take me out to the ball game? Nah, I'd rather catch it on the Web.

USA Today Baseball www.usatoday.com/sports/mlb.htm

A direct line to *USA Today*'s superior coverage of America's favorite pastime, with all of the news, recaps, box scores, and game-by-game match-up analysis laid out in the reassuringly familiar format of the favorite newspaper. Click on the game listings on the right side of the page to see mid-inning updates that refresh every two minutes for games currently in progress.

Baseball Links www.baseball-links.com © *d*

The homepage of John Skilton's Baseball Links proclaims, "If you can't find what you're looking for here, then it probably doesn't exist," and that's probably true. It provides 7,000 links to baseball sites around the Web, and the selections aren't limited to the major leagues, either. There are also sites devoted to the minors, international leagues, high school and college ball, and cards and collectibles. Extremely well organized and tremendous in scope.

NCAABaseball.com www.ncaabaseball.com

The "ping!" of the aluminum bat means it's time for college baseball, and where better to go for information on the latest horsehide happenings than the official NCAA source? Here, you can read up on the latest games, see photos and box scores, or get down in the dirt with TotalCast broadcasts of high-profile games. There are also plenty of opportunities to nab merchandise, and ticket information is provided for the College World Series.

National Baseball Hall of Fame www.baseballhalloffame.org ©

If you can't make it to Cooperstown to check out baseball's historic hall, the least you can do is visit it online. The official site of the Baseball Hall of Fame is a nostalgic tribute, with archived video footage and news clippings recalling the greats who once bestrode America's baseball diamonds. But it's not just fond memories—serious research can be done in the Hall's offline library through the ABNER online card catalog.

Fastball www.fastball.com

According to Yogi Berra, "Baseball is 90 percent mental. The other half is physical." Had he lived to see it, Berra would have loved the info on Fastball, where pull-down menus of American or National League teams give instant access to statistics, news, and On the Dial radio broadcasts on the current baseball season. Also check the bulletin boards and chat rooms, or head to Foul Pole for lighthearted quotes from other former greats.

Slurve.net www.slurve.net

E-zine attitude meets the grand old game of baseball at Slurve.net, a fan-run site dedicated to major league play. But while the tone may be irreverent, the depth of coverage is no laughing matter. Slurve.net serves up editorial content chock full of opinion and analysis, with unique features like links to local team coverage and reviews of other baseball-related sites. If you're feeling punchy, visit the forums to communicate with other diamond-minded smart alecks.

Baseball Almanac www.baseball-almanac.com

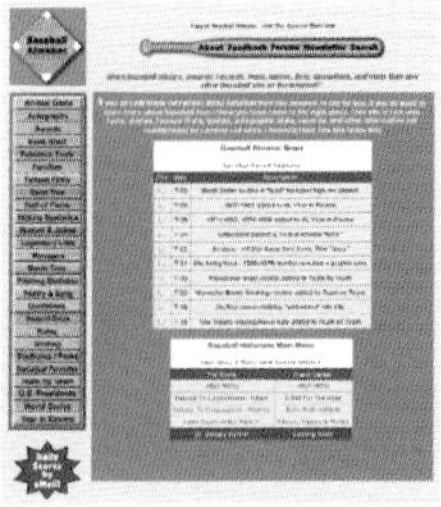

Unless you know everything, you'll find something you don't know here. How about the words to "Casey at the Bat"? The members of the .400 batting average club? All that is and could be baseball trivia is at the Baseball Almanac, a fan-run site that is mind-blowingly comprehensive. Stats, of course, are everywhere, but there's also a lot of "unofficial" info (like a rundown of the good and the bad in baseball cinema) for aficionados looking to do more than crunch numbers.

Baseball Weekly www.totalbaseballweekly.com

The magazine that's in every baseball fanatic's bathroom is now on every baseball fanatic's PC thanks to *Total Baseball Weekly*'s Web site. The electronic version deemphasizes the usual stat tracking and scoreboard in favor of analysis and commentary, but the depth is the same—articles dig into who was injured during the All-Star break, great interleague rivalries, and anything else that catches the columnists' eyes. But if it's stats you want, link to the new Daily section—it has the very latest scores and boxes.

Baseball America Online
www.baseballamerica.com

Whether you're looking for news on the best in high school baseball or an analysis of the worst trades in the bigs, there's something for you at this site. The usual array of stats and scores (for all levels of play) is complemented by analysis and commentary from the people responsible for Baseball America Online's print counterpart. The e-commerce side was not functional at press time.

Negro League Baseball Dot Com www.negroleaguebaseball.com

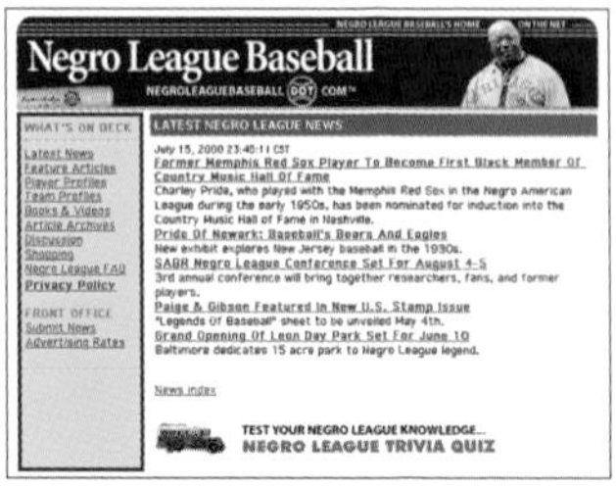

John Henry Lloyd and Josh Gibson never got the attention they deserved in their time, but they and their fellow players achieve some semblance of immortality at this site dedicated to Negro League play. Statistics are scarce due to the lack of solid record keeping, but the lore lives on through athlete profiles, news updates on past greats, and editorial content dedicated to remembering the great baseball played by these men.

minorleaguebaseball.com www.minorleaguebaseball.com

Minor league baseball is known for being the most fun you can have at the ballpark these days, and the farm teams' official site brings that hustle directly to your desktop. Every league in every class from Rookie to the near-big-league action of AAA is covered, with scores, schedules, and highlights—even the attendance figures of the last game. The news archives aren't kept up as well as they could be, so use the popular bulletin boards to learn the latest.

MLBtalk www.sportstalk.com/mlb

For anyone who likes coverage deeper than a Mark McGwire homer. You can find standard fare like up-to-date stats and scores for every team in the league, but this site takes that extra step by providing news stories directly from each team as well. Check out individual profiles and analysis of players battling for specific positions on particular teams. Like a game-winning bloop single, the look's not that pretty, but it more than gets the job done.

New York Yankees www.yankees.com

Love 'em or hate 'em, the New York Yankees are one of the most tradition-rich, storied organizations in baseball. The official site does this legacy proud with up-to-date stats, player profiles, plenty of pictures (including downloadable desktop themes), and a complete history of the club. Live chat forums let fans gab about the Bronx Bombers' prospects, and an online box office lets them check game schedules and book tickets.

Star Struck's At the Yard www.attheyard.com ©

Today's minor league prospects are tomorrow's major league stars, and At the Yard would like to introduce them to you. The site features journal entries posted by more than 20 players—reading them, users can see the game (and everything that comes with it) through the competitive eyes of the baseballers. Coaches and team physicians from around the minors also chime in with training advice—check out the RealVideo instructional videos and the expert advice in the Community section.

Little League Online www.littleleague.org

Little League is still about as American as apple pie. Parent-coaches will appreciate Little League Online's articles that not only cover general game and league info, but also dish out interesting features on things like baseball summer camp and game rules and the organization's history. Kids will love the section specially tailored to their needs, with word play, puzzles, and info on free admission to the Little League Museum.

The Baseball Heckle Depot www.heckledepot.com ⓪

"You're supposed to be a pitcher, not a bowler!" "You couldn't throw a party!" MLB players will hate Heckle Depot, but who's to say the pampered pros don't need to be taken down a notch or two? More than 600 categorized taunts and jeers make this clunky but feature-rich site the perfect resource for the opinionated and vocal fan—stop here for chants, user-submitted stories, player-specific zingers, and a top ten list of the best players to heckle.

Dodgers.com www.dodgers.com

Fans who have ever caught Dodger fever will feel they've entered their own blue heaven when they visit the team's official Web site. An opening Flash movie on the history of Dodger baseball gets the nostalgic juices flowing and the mood is maintained with an archive of classic radio broadcast clips, video footage, and images. There's plenty of information about the modern-day Dodgers as well, with stats, player profiles, press links, and a store full of merchandise.

Atlanta Braves www.atlantabraves.com

The Atlanta Braves, for many years a laughing stock of the majors, have been no joke for the past decade, achieving much on-field success. The team's Web presence is equally impressive, with multimedia features, a team history, and player-related features to whet fans' appetites. The usual stats and news updates are in effect, and there's a definite emphasis on community, with forums and chat in addition to details on various charitable foundations. The tomahawk chop, thankfully, is nowhere to be seen.

Chicago Cubs www.cubs.com ©

The Internet home for all things Cubbies. Stats and game-by-game coverage keep you updated on the trials and triumphs of Chicago's favorite team, while an e-commerce storefront steps in with team outfits and gear. Multimedia is all over the place, with video highlights and profiles on Cubs players past and present. The coolest feature by far is the CubsCam, an interactive webcam that offers a panoramic view of Wrigley Field.

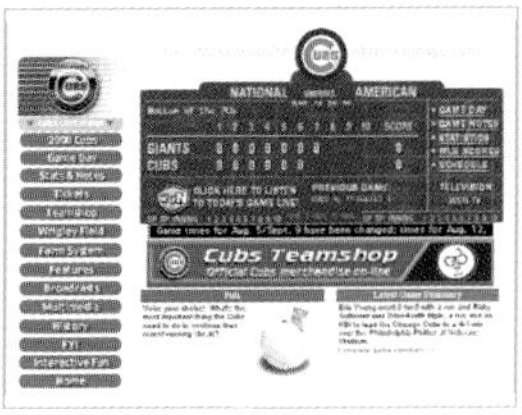

NBA.com www.nba.com Ⓒ ⓓ

Affording a better (and cheaper) glimpse into pro basketball action than those $200 court-side seats, NBA.com has a minute-by-minute Live Scoreboard that keeps track of current games, and a news section that highlights yesterday's match-up. Each team has its own page, or "theater," where news, audio clips, stats, and game schedules are listed. Don't miss the great Sights & Sounds multimedia area—it has QuickTime video of the top plays of the week and a video archive of history-making shots.

WNBA.com www.wnba.com

Yolanda Griffith, Rebecca Lobo, and other girls with game are featured on the official site of the Women's National Basketball Association. Each player gets a page with game highlights, stats, personal and injury details, and a complete game log; there is also a printable version for those who keep track of such things. The site also has the stats, news, and Q & A chat sessions with players you would expect to find on an official site, as well as a multimedia area with RealPlayer video of season highlights and nail-biting buzzer-beaters.

FindHoops.com www.findhoops.com

Hoops fanatics will say "Yahoo!" when they see the sheer number of links on this basketball portal. High school, college, CBA, WNBA, and international play are all covered in addition to the obvious NBA angle, and many of the links are accompanied by thorough descriptions of the site's content. Not all of the sites are of the highest quality, but there are several alternatives if you don't like a particular listing.

FinalFour.net www.finalfour.net

At FinalFour.net, it's all about madness—of the March variety. Once a year, hoops fans everywhere rip out that all-important page of the sports section (the brackets). Before you make your bets for next season's NCAA tournament, check this site for stats, scouting reports, and news updates. Real-time webcasts take you all the way from the round of 64 to the Final Four and championship game.

Shaq www.shaq.com

At 7' 1", 310, Shaquille O'Neal is bigger than the rest of the NBA, but how does he measure up online? Find out at his official site. There's lots of multimedia action here, like game footage, clips from Shaq's albums, and a run-down on his career with the Lakers and his life off court. And yes, the man himself does show up occasionally for chat.

Remember the ABA www.remembertheaba.com

Remember when the balls were red, white, and blue? Remember where Doctor J got his start? This site does. It's a fond, fan-created tribute to the American Basketball Association, with stats and scores taking a backseat to nostalgic looks at the freewheeling atmosphere surrounding the league. Hit the Fashion Guide to see 101 muttonchops, take the Trivia Quiz, or read about the rivalry between the NBA and its outlaw cousin.

Basketball Hall of Fame www.hoophall.com

This Hall of Fame is lesser known than its Cooperstown cousin, but its site is nearly as exciting as the game of basketball itself. In addition to the usual list of inductees and articles on the history of the sport, you're also treated to player profiles, columns, analysis of the game—past and present—and interactive games to test your knowledge and skills. The graphics-intensive site may tax low-bandwidth connections, but it's worth the download time if you're looking to relive roundball glory.

HoopsBoards.com www.hoopsboards.com

Sit around a bar yakking about last week's basketball game, or hit the Boards for smart, lively discussion on NBA and college play… Hmm, tough choice. HoopsBoards.com hosts very active forums and boards on a cornucopia of topics, with a network of team- and player-specific sites at hand to fuel the fire. Hit the Daily Dose link for some meaty news to use, and then look for the little flaming folders to see which threads are getting the most heated discussion.

NCAA Basketball www.ncaabasketball.net

You can almost hear the pep band at NCAA Basketball, the official home of men's and women's college hoops. Simple, drop-down menus offer access to scores and news on every team, but registered members can save a personal My Team page to go directly to customized reports based on the team they follow. The Game section sports lighter fare, like cool "virtual tours" of famous arenas like Florida's O Dome, and the stats of all-time great players.

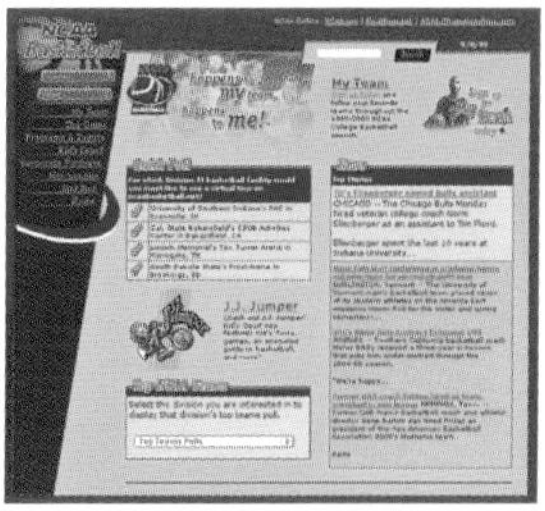

HoopsTV.com www.hoopstv.com ⓓ

Take the irreverence (and scantily clad women) of *Maxim* magazine and marry it to SportsLine-quality coverage of basketball, and what do you have? HoopsTV.com, where the not-so-serious tone doesn't do justice to the scope of news and features provided. Video and audio commentary on high schools, camps, and street ball tourneys accompany the standard NBA coverage, all packed into an entertainment-center interface. Launch the remote control window for the easiest access to everything.

Hooplife www.hooplife.com ©

Court's in session at Hooplife, where you'll find news, features, and games dealing with Dr. Naismith's greatest creation. The slant is definitely toward a young audience, but the scope of information (everything from college ball to the NBA to international leagues) makes this a central location for anyone looking for more than the latest scores. Nutrition and training guidelines might make it possible for you, too, to be featured here someday.

Gballmag.com www.gballmag.com

Go to WNBA.com for stats and schedules, but come to Gballmag.com

to meet the ladies behind USA, WNBA, NCAA, and high school basketball. New player profiles are posted nearly every week, letting users take a peek inside the heads of superstars like Kristin Folkl and Sheryl Swoopes. The tone sometimes verges on fluffy—the sports gear shopping mall has more than one type of hair scrunchy—but the site does manage to maintain enthusiasm without being elitist.

Sportstation cityhoops www.cityhoops.com

Some would say the best basketball in America isn't played in the NBA, but on the blacktop of playgrounds all around the country. Run by Sportstation, this site takes you to the streets where the action is hottest with lots of user-submitted news and features. Information on streetball tournaments and leagues is nice, but pales in comparison to the listing of the best playgrounds on which to play anywhere in the world. Hoop it up.

The Basketball Highway www.bbhighway.com

The road to coaching success can be long and hard, but you can take a shortcut with the Basketball Highway, a comprehensive resource for basketball gurus. The scope of resources is pretty broad, ranging from a dissection of the triangle offense to reviews of stat-tracking software. The smallish font and somewhat convoluted navigation can be a hassle, but, lucky you, in this case smaller text means longer and more in-depth articles.

Michael Jordan www.jordan.sportsline.com
Catch some Air—Air Jordan, that is—at this official home of the new owner of the Washington Wizards (we've heard he was also a decent basketball player). Thanks to CBS SportsLine, you can relive the greatest moments of Jordan's career in pictures and video, play Shockwave basketball against him, and even get tips from his personal trainer. You'll be glad to know that #23 does take questions over email, though our repeated requests for an endorsement were, for some reason, ignored.

CBAHoops.com www.cbahoops.com
Unlike minor league baseball, the NBA's developmental league has never really shone. Now it gets a fair shake thanks to CBAHoops.com, where you can read history of the Continental Basketball Association before digging into news and scores for teams like the Rockford Lightning and the Sioux Falls Sky Force. Find out what players can do before they reach the NBA, then track the progress of CBA alums throughout their careers. Order tickets for every team online or let live webcasts bring the action right to your computer.

Official Site of the Harlem Globetrotters
www.harlemglobetrotters.com

Like the Globetrotters themselves, this site whips up a lot of compelling action. The graphics and sound effects are great, as is the extensive history lesson on the team. This site is very dedicated to promoting the many cultural, economic, and social contributions of the team, both past and present. Highly entertaining, but not as fun as attending an actual game.

bodybuilding

HardcoreBodybuilding.com www.hardcorebodybuilding.com

A 5,000 calories-a-day diet is only the first step to "getting big." According to the instructions on Hardcore Bodybuilding, you'll also need the training how-tos and exercises listed here. Though decidedly low-tech, the site does offer some of the best bodybuilding instructions we've seen online, and plenty of pictures for inspiration. Now if they would just explain how to ingest 2.5g of protein per pound of body-weight every day without having to guzzle twelve cans of tuna fish.

Musclehedz www.musclehedz.com
Picture lots of big, muscular men with tiny, tiny heads and you've got the idea behind Muclehedz, John Gleneicki's bodybuilding comic strip. You'll find several funny new strips each week on this cluttered site, and an archive of nearly 100 past favorites in the Gallery. The site also offers a biography of the artist, e-cards and screensavers, and lots of heavy-handed product promotion.

SteelFitness.Com www.steelfitness.com

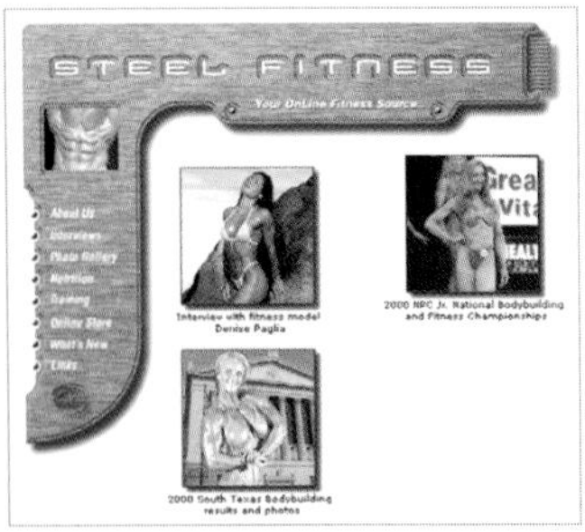

Would you be surprised that many hard-core bodybuilders wake up at 6:30 a.m.? SteelFitness.com interviews four different athletes each month, delving into their daily routine, favorite foods, and other personal details as well as their training tips. The site also houses a large gallery of photo and video clips from tournaments like the Arnold Classic. But for detailed guidance on your own routine, you'll have to surf elsewhere—the training and nutrition sections are currently very limited.

getcut.com www.getcut.com

Brawn and brains—getcut.com sells every kind of supplement on the market, backed up by a research library that explains why you would want any of them. You'll find a link to the FDA guide to supplements, a vitamin and mineral guide, and a few worthwhile articles among other essentials. Learn how to overcome those fitness plateaus, or find out how much is too much protein, and then stock up. Orders that hit the $50 mark are shipped for free.

Muscle & Fitness www.muscle-fitness.com

Surfing the Web usually isn't the best way to stay physically fit, so it's good to have sites like Muscle & Fitness to show the way to buff bods. Visitors to this site have access to in-depth training tips for all parts of the body as well as sports medicine information offered by experts in the field. If the thought of a good sweat isn't enough to get you inspired, take a look at some of the hot bodies in the photo gallery.

boxing

World Wide Houseofboxing.com www.houseofboxing.com

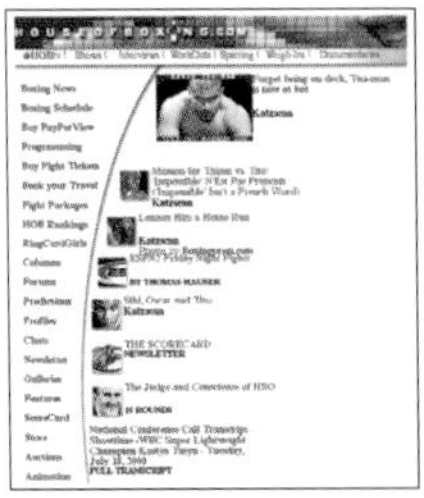

Nifty to look at and easy to search, Houseofboxing.com gives fans everything they need to know about rankings, weigh-ins, fight schedules, and spotlight matches. It frequently adds interviews with the likes of De La Hoya and Roy Jones Jr. to its list of videos, and covers who, exactly, bit off what in the most recent bout. There's also a page dedicated to each of the major figures in international boxing.

Showtime Championship Boxing Online
www.sho.com/scboxing

It's a knockout—the plentitude of pugilistic particulars at this site would be enough to make even Don King blush. Read about approaching bouts, then score the matches at home with Showtime's Interactive Event Coverage. The network's top experts weigh in with analysis before, during, and after all the top fights, and the Hit Report brings it to you in style with the latest news and hard-hitting multimedia.

Womens Boxing Archive Network www.womenboxing.com

J'Marie Moore, Laila Ali, Irichelle Duran—many of boxing's First Daughters have become fighters themselves, and this site has their profiles along with those of 70 other women. The hard stats and rankings are peppered with engaging behind-the-scenes looks at the athletes' preparations and columns that uncover the seamy underbelly of the sport. (Who knew some mismatches were intentional?) And while you won't find much video here, there are three separate galleries of photographs from the fights.

Ringside www.ringside.com

You wanna fight? Ringside sells every type of equipment for before, during, and after the match—including jump ropes, gloves, mouth guards, and ice packs, to name a few. A heavyweight selection of Web specials makes buying online especially worthwhile—a $50 speed bag was priced at $25 when we visited. The site also offers some helpful information, like the contact name and phone number for every state's USA Boxing representative, though we did encounter a few dead links.

HBO Boxing www.hbo.com/boxing

Sure, your first choice is to catch the action ringside. But for those who can't be there, HBO's online boxing correspondents detail the action round by round—right down to "Frans managed a brave smile"—with a few photos of the fight and plenty of stats on punches landed and averted. Peer into the Boxing After Dark link for great moments in HBO boxing since 1975.

FightNews.com www.fightnews.com

FightNews.com may be a welterweight among bigger sports sites, but it's got speed on its side. It beats bigger sites like ESPN.com and CNNsi to stories by hours, newspapers by a day, and magazines by weeks. Skeptics can actually click and compare—the site provides links to around 40 other boxing columns and commentaries. Coverage here also includes fights the mainstream press usually pays no attention to, all with a healthy entertainment and human-interest angle.

BoxingPress.com www.boxingpress.com

News flash: it turns out Lennox Lewis isn't gay, after all. He says he just doesn't go out in public with his girlfriend because he cares about her privacy. BoxingPress.com is as gossipy as it is useful, but it is useful—international rankings, schedules, and some solid editorial content are the foundation for the not-so-serious aspects. Now it just needs to fill out the lighter sections; when browsing the Ring Marvels and Mythical Matchups sections, we simply wanted more.

OscarDeLaHoya.com www.oscardelahoya.com ⓓ

The pretty boy of boxing? Say what you will, De La Hoya does have a pretty Web site, with cool music and amazing Shockwave animation. A fast connection is a must for viewing, but if you've got the speed, Oscardelahoya.com will dazzle. Archived video clips, bios, and match news make the site a must-see for casual fans and die-hards alike.

coaching & instruction

AthletesVillage.com www.athletesvillage.com ⓞ

It takes a village to build an athlete, and if that village is virtual, so much the better. Coaching and instruction are the main attractions here, with advice coming from certified experts, community members, and top-flight athletes. Shop the site's partners, stay informed on upcoming athletic events with user-friendly calendars, and track competitive goals using Net-based tools. It's always easier to work out with companions and with AthletesVillage.com, the entire Web is your training partner.

SportsID.com www.sportsid.com ©

Remember those cheesy instructional sports videos starring professional athletes you used to watch as a kid? This site is like that, but it's free and totally free of cheese. Here you can find educational video clips that teach everything from archery to yoga, configured for a variety of media players and Internet connections. Hosts range from Hall of Fame talent like Bill Walton to lesser-known luminaries like table tennis guru Dennis Davis.

Coach's Edge www.coachesedge.com © ⓓ

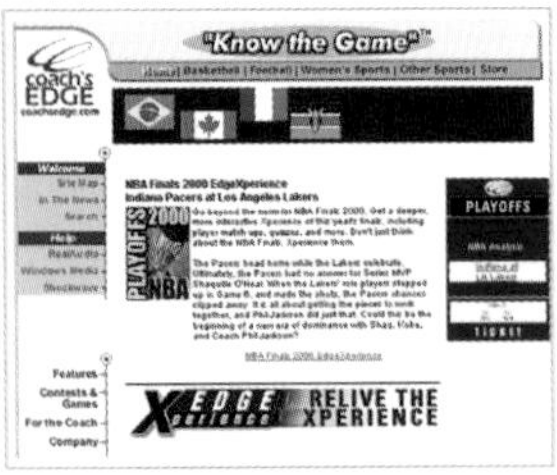

Who just checks the scores anymore? Here, you can become an expert in your favorite sports while keeping updated on the latest happenings. The Coach breaks down the plays that make the evening highlights, using nifty Flash animation to show why things worked, and why the rest didn't. The focus here is on basketball and football, but you'll also find pages on women's sports and sub-features on NASCAR, leaving you little reason not to engage.

lifetips.com www.lifetips.com

Hey, buddy…need a tip? This network has been dubbed "the online owner's manual for your life" because it compiles a large collection of little hints and tricks to help you live better. Tips are subdivided into more than 230 subsites, each one addressing a specific topic like sports and exercise, dating, and even poison control. You'll get advice from appointed "Gurus" as well as users, and only occasionally is the advice not astute.

mysportsguru.com www.mysportsguru.com ⓓ ⓞ

If you're learning tennis, baseball, or golf, you could do worse than getting instruction written and approved by the likes of Nick Bollettieri, Cal Ripken, and David Leadbetter. mysportsguru.com aims to bring expert insight to your desktop on baseball, basketball, bowling, fly-fishing, inline skating, golf, and tennis, pairing written instructions with animated lessons, drills, and Q & A. Check the recommended skill level on each lesson, so you won't mistakenly attempt a backward power slide before you can tie your skates.

ActiveLog www.activelog.com

Keeping an exercise journal is said to be one of the best ways to stay motivated. ActiveLog is a free, Web-based fitness diary that allows registered users to set goals and track their progress in a variety of fitness activities like running, weight training, and inline skating. A personalized calendar and workout planner are just two of the tools that each user gets. ActiveLog will even be the voice in your ear (well, email) reminding you to get going after periods of inactivity.

college sports

Recruit www.recruitzone.com

For $45, a high school athlete can make it big at this NCAA-backed clearinghouse that connects high school players with college coaches. Players fill out an online application that details their academic and sporting careers, and the site forwards it to scouts at campuses across the nation. Also look here for tips and strategies for succeeding at the college level, straight from pros who've been there.

FANSonly.com www.fansonly.com

Created for fanatic devotees of the NCAA, FANSonly.com is also open to non-initiates looking for news, articles, and up-to-the-minute stats on games. There's an impressive section devoted to scouting and signing updates on the next generation of MVPs; high school athletes looking to get noticed can log profiles and get advice on how to stand out for the scouts. Got some choice words for pathetic players and coaches? Post your sideline epithets on this site and tell them how they should play.

CollegeInsider.com www.collegeinsider.com ©

You know those people who seem to know everything about college sports, from general rankings to the high school player most likely to play baseball for Washington State next year? They use this Web site. Detailed information on individual players, coaches, schools, and teams is packed into the news stories, interactive polls, and feature articles this site offers. The focus is exclusively on the men's half of college basketball, football, and baseball, with the most attention going to the sport currently in season.

NCAAChampionships.com www.ncaachampionships.com

From the umbrella association that oversees 20 college sports (football all the way down to fencing) comes a catchall resource for championship information. It's got voluminous stats and stories on big games and rivalries, often with live "photocasts" from events currently taking place. Helpful extras include a TV schedule, links to individual team pages, and a listing of college mascots.

TotalCollegeSports.com www.totalcollegesports.com

Because beer bellies do not good athletes make, skip the neighborhood sports bar and get your college basketball and football news from the definitive online source. While it only covers those two sports (making "total" something of a misnomer), the site has views on every team imaginable, as well as stories on specific coaches and players. Because of its relationship to TotalSports, the site also has a link to the live game coverage (called "totalcasts") of its parent site.

Fightsongs.com www.fightsongs.com

Oskee Wow Wow. The Buckeye Battlecry. They stir your heart, those old college fight songs. As the name suggests, this site is a database devoted to the patriotic tunes of colleges across the nation. Pick your conference, click on any title, and wait out the quick download to hear the anthem of your alma mater blasting through your PC's speakers. Not much else here besides the audio files, but for nostalgia's sake, we'll take it.

NCAA Online www.ncaa.org ⓒ ⓓ ⓞ

Though the portal to the NCAA network of sports sites is an excellent way to connect to individual sites on college sports and tournaments, its real utility comes from the official information it makes available to student athletes. All of the essential guidelines have been outlined in a sidebar that stretches along two screens, including gambling, amateurism, drug testing, and more—if you don't check here, you may never know that caffeine is just as regulated as marijuana and cocaine.

National Association of Intercollegiate Athletics www.naia.org

Colleges like Montana State and Kansas Wesleyan belong to this step-brother of the NCAA, so for sports info on these schools, this is the place to go. While the design suffers from a low-tech aesthetic and lack of graphics, it does break down stats, championship updates, and news for the full range of college sports, even providing some interesting articles during the off-season.

iHigh.com www.ihigh.com ©

Cliques are for kids; clicking at iHigh.com, on the other hand, is for the hip and tuned-in high school netizen. Venture beyond the Who's Who of your school to see how peers from the rest of the country are competing in basketball, cheerleading, soccer, tennis, and more (with separate sites devoted to each sport). Or, create a free page for your own school and pack it with the latest sports news, schedules, player bios, and even a nifty sports ticker.

SportsUniversity.com www.sportsuniversity.com

SportsUniversity.com gives you college sports from the campus perspective. Besides the standard coverage of recent games (including audio highlights), the site spotlights upcoming players and offers a peek inside some of their journals. Air your thoughts and predictions for how they'll perform this season in the forum, or link through to an individual team page for deeper content. Though the site covers almost all college sports, basketball and football get the most attention.

Varsity.com www.varsity.com

You might think a Web site devoted to cheerleading is silly (because you think cheerleading is silly), but judging by the information here, these girls have game. This site is an online cheer community that combines advice on the undeniably gymnastic side of the sport with some health, fashion, and fitness features. Registered members can personalize the homepage with their own calendar, or set up a squad page to connect with their coach and teammates.

Big Ten Conference www.bigten.org ⓓ

A sports site dedicated to the big guys—Penn State, Michigan State—the real sports schools. While a mass of television game listings makes it tempting to log off and turn on the tube, the extensive information on every single school and sport in the conference makes it equally difficult to pull your eyes away. Especially magnetic is the entire subsite devoted to championships and tournaments; post-tournament quotes and gamecasts are just two features it contains.

Big East Conference www.bigeast.org

14 schools, 21 sports, and more than 5,000 athletes put the "big" in the Big East conference. The conference's Web site is similarly expansive, with 20 years worth of information on each of the sports and separate photo galleries for each of the football and basketball teams (men's and women's). Live cybercasts of the games are also available, though they only entail audio and text commentary—if you'd like to see the action, a television schedule is provided.

ABC Championship Bowl Series Online www.abccfb.com
ABC's online partnership with the ESPN network makes this site a convenient gateway to both the television and online coverage of college football. Browse around the homepage for commentary from the station's announcers, or click into Conferences and Teams for the specific breakdown of how a school is performing this season (or last, if the new season has yet to start). The site excels in its coverage of bowl games, so if the time is right, you'll find that here as well.

FanaticZone.com www.fanaticzone.com ©
This fan site for the Southern Conference proffers the latest stories about schools like Alabama and Ole Miss, pages devoted to men and women's track and other so-called lesser sports, downloadable audio interviews with coaches and players, and—get this—animated recaps of basketball games. Sign up for the newsletter to get it all, including clips of the interviews, delivered to your inbox.

cycling

Bicycling www.bicycling.com

So you don't have Lance Armstrong's maniac calves. Don't worry. Bicycling has info for those who have yet to buy their first bike as well as those who've already booked a hotel for the next Tour de France. Get specs on 2,800 different bikes, repair how-tos, and a new training program each week for both recreational and racing cyclists.

Pete's BikIndex www.bikindex.com
A no-nonsense cycling resource that's packed with lists of training groups, places to buy bike equipment online, and info for folks looking for riding partners. Not the most visually exciting spot on the Web, Pete's BikIndex makes up in content what it lacks in aesthetics.

BMXonline.com www.bmxonline.com
To get a more insider perspective on the gritty world of BMX, you'd have to sit on a biker's lap. The site for *Ride* and *Snap* magazines is put together by some goofy guys who keep extremely close tabs on product releases and reviews, race results, and who broke his foot in last week's race. They even cover things that might be going on—the Rumormill section has a mudslide of speculation and gossip straight from the track.

RoadbikeReview.com www.roadbikereview.com
A consumer-driven Web site is only as good as the community behind it, and judging by the number of product reviews at RoadbikeReview.com, there's a horde of dedicated cyclists out there backing up this one. Hundreds of user comments point out how various bikes and accessories compare, with halls of Fame and Shame for the best and worst of the bunch. You'll also want to check this site's extensive classifieds (with bikes ranging from $400 to $1300), and the What's Hot link if you're in the market.

VeloNews.com www.velonews.com

Like a *New York Times* for the cycling world, VeloNews offers an authoritative (though not necessarily innovative) source for news. You'll get all the stories of record in long, well-educated strokes, though seeing all of them requires scrolling down for five minutes. When we visited, there were more than 30 articles on specific races like the Tour de France. But because the site falls under the umbrella of Greatoutdoors.com, some of the links may lead you off topic.

Adventure Cycling Association www.adv-cycling.org

"Inspiring people to ride bicycles since 1976" is this site's motto. To that end they serve up rider stories on group bicycling trips, equipment news, and info on the association itself. The best part of the site is its route map—the ACA has researched and mapped out bike routes throughout the country, creating an easy-to-access archive for everyone from the day-tripper to the cross-country enthusiast.

Bike Ride Online www.bikeride.com

If you're interested in a relatively obscure bike race in Oregon, here is where you'll find the commentary. This site is a clearinghouse for cycling news that relies on regional cycling sites to make its coverage some of the widest we've seen. The feature content is similarly massive, and similarly reliant on outside sources, with links for famous bikers, routes, equipment reviews, and sites of interest to the mountain biking, track cycling, and racing communities.

Mountain Bike Daily www.mountainbike.com

Who is Spaz boy and will he find a new girlfriend? Find out by clicking onto this site's Ship of Fools section. Besides wacky columns and columnists, Mountain Bike Daily serves up an interesting assortment of product tests (performed daily) and updates, racing news, and forums.

DirtWorld.com www.dirtworld.com

According to DirtWorld.com, the key to unlocking your potential for face-smearing speed is simply this: don't use the brakes. But for less daring mountain bikers, the sport's all-inclusive online community also covers safer ways to improve performance, with equipment reviews, a Repair Stand, and tips from the pros. Check the Bike Store for replacement parts and classifieds.

MTBInfo www.mtbinfo.com

There's no flash and dazzle design here, but for mountain bikers who want a wealth of information, MTBInfo will suffice. You'll find a massive list of trails for every state, each with a rating based on level of aerobic workout, scenic quality, and traffic. When you're done with your workout, peruse the site's bike maintenance tips, product news, and bulletin boards to exchange tips with other riders.

mtbReview.com www.mtbr.com

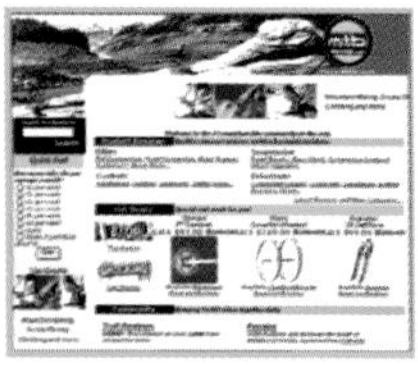

An arm of ConsumerReview.com's empire, this combination shopping mall and encyclopedia for mountain bikers covers both products and destinations. The product portion has a huge number of volunteer-contributed postings on bikes and accessories—we saw 130 reviews on one specific brand of shock alone. The trails database covers 13,000 routes nationwide, detailing literally which turns to take if you're a beginner or someone who's been riding for years. The community aspect also makes it a great source for tech talk, photos, and chat.

Dirt Rag Magazine www.dirtragmag.com

What *Dirt Rag Magazine*'s site lacks in depth, it makes up for in soul. So, while you might expect a more robust archive from a publication that's put out 80 issues, you'll be impressed by the activity in the message boards (literally hundreds of posts daily), the user-submitted photos, and some honest and well-informed writing. To make the most of the content (without paying for a $14 annual subscription), sign up for the eNewsletter and mine the enormous links section of products and resources.

trekbikes.com www.trekbikes.com ©

This site combines the corporate feel of a company homepage with the added flair of an enthusiast's pet project. Here you'll find great graphics of Trek bikes, with plenty of descriptions and stats on specific parts. You'll also have access to profiles of racers and stories on the race, the bikers, and their gear. Note: though features are plentiful, you'll need added applications to view many of them.

bike.com www.bike.com ©

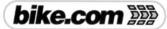

Walking the line between e-tailer and community site, bike.com sports a simple interface that can get you the full range of bikes, frames, and accessories along with a plethora of race information. The Tour de France maps and profiles (in the Experience section) are particularly good, as is the entire subsite devoted to cool children's equipment. But don't spend time on the buggy community chat link, which wouldn't load after repeated tries.

Cannondale www.cannondale.com

While every link eventually leads to the underwriters, would you be here if you didn't want to buy a bike? The slick, corporate Cannondale site has the official info on its bikes and parts (both bicycles and motorcycles), as well as warranty conditions and details on any current sales. So while there is other stuff to be had (tips on biking, race news, questionnaires, etc.), we suggest using it for the select-a-bike tool and then the dealer locator.

Schwinn www.schwinn.com
Schwinn's corporate site is kind of like their bikes: big, red, and retro. So if you're looking to shop online for the "Rocket 88" and "The Classic"—wheels for zipping around the block—this is the place to do it. Schwinn also sells bicycle parts and fitness equipment (they're up with the times). Best of all for consumers, the site sports a long how-to page that answers any and all questions about ordering products over the Net.

bikestore.com www.bikestore.com
You're cycling through the urban jungle that is your backyard and you blow your front tire. Where's the closest bike store? If you can find a computer and go online, this site will fix your problem. Not only does the site sell its own gear (complete with product reviews and buying guides), it features a unique search engine that finds bike stores in your area.

events

Olympics.com www.olympics.com
For anyone who missed the latest Olympic match-ups or who wants to relive highlights of Games past, Olympics.com is the place to visit. Read up on the athletes or research the event's history. The torch section is particularly fascinating, and details the 50 different modes of transportation used to carry the torch to the Sydney Olympics, including a train, a camel, a surf-lifesaving boat, and a scuba diver.

Ironmanlive.com www.ironmanlive.com ⓓ
The champion of triathlon sites, this one covers the biggest event in the sport, and it does so live. Besides course maps, rules for the running, swimming, and biking events and the history of the course, the site offers live coverage of Ironman competitions in California, Australia, and New Zealand. Also find: in-depth stories about the ins and outs of the race, and training tips for mind and body at the Ironman Institute.

CitySearch www.citysearch.com ©
So many cities, so much to do! CitySearch gives you the hottest sports event listings for more than 50 cities in the United States and abroad—each city has its own massive subsite with local college and professional team events. There's valuable info for natives as well as out-of-towners, loads of columns and interactive boards, and the kind of writing that's in-the-know without being snotty.

Ticketmaster.com www.ticketmaster.com ©

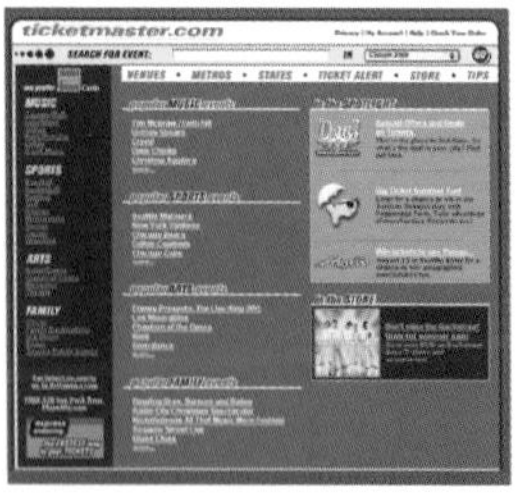

Ticketmaster remains the biggest ticketing agency in the U.S. That's both good and bad. On the upside, you can get tickets to nearly any large sporting event in the nation, from the Cubs' next game to the WWF Smackdown. On the downside, you'll have to pay Ticketmaster's considerable "convenience" charge every time. Still, for selection and reliability, the site can't be outdone.

Tickets.com www.tickets.com

Whether you're willing to fly halfway around the world to see Pete Sampras or are just too lazy to drag your butt over to the local ticket kiosk, this Web site can help. Ticket-hungry sports fans will find tickets to sporting events, cruises, concerts, and museums. If you don't see what you want, head for the auction page, where you can do battle for the last World Series ticket in the continental U.S.

Churchill Downs www.kentuckyderby.com

Few sports spectacles match the pageantry of the first leg of horse racing's Triple Crown, the Kentucky Derby. Churchill Downs is home to the Derby and this official site is a wonderful resource for information on races past and present. Bet the Races links up to the current day's race card with real-time odds and track reports, racing news, and a primer for beginning betters. Want to know who won Derby 112? The stats archive lists each race result all the way back to 1875.

Goodwill Games www.goodwillgames.org

Originally founded in 1986 to foster friendliness between the U.S. and the USSR, the Goodwill Games have gone online. This snappy Web site features a huge archive of video and results from the last Games and a growing list of athletes and contact information for the upcoming ones. More feature content can be had in the GETset newsletter, though the tone is decidedly aimed at corporate readers. Watch the site get better and better as the ticker along the top counts down the days to competition.

Special Olympics www.specialolympics.org

The official site for the Special Olympics is a font of contact numbers and volunteer information for anyone wanting to get involved with the events—as sponsor, coach, family member, or athlete. More expansive feature articles can be found in Spirit, the organization's e-zine, though perhaps the most engaging part of the site is the explanations of specific Special Olympic events, from equestrian sports to soccer to bocce ball.

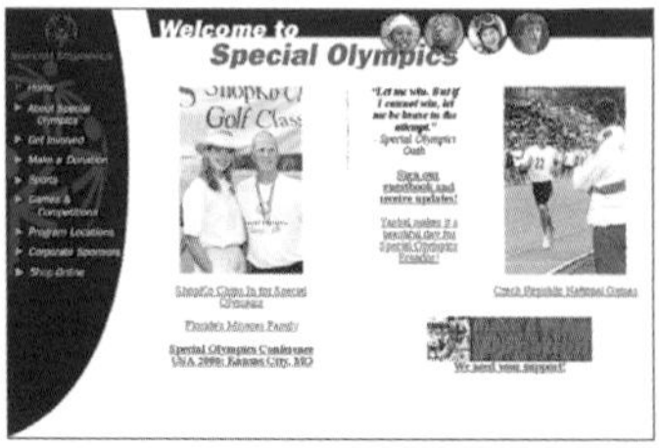

NBCOlympics.com www.nbcolympics.com
Breaking news and insider views on every Olympic sport from badminton to archery, synchronized swimming to the perennially entertaining rhythmic gymnastics; Quokka Sports' Web savvy and NBC's event coverage are a winning pair. New feature articles and headlines are posted daily, but the site really shines in its first-person accounts of the action. Live event coverage, athletes' diaries, audio interview transcripts, and loads of state-of-the-art media files let you know what it's like to participate in the Games.

SportTicket.com www.sportticket.com
Stand in line to score those Bulls tickets? No thanks. This eBay of sports tickets is a forum where buyers and sellers can freely post wanted and for sale ads for tickets to baseball, football, hockey, basketball, racing events and more. A handy search function makes it simple to find a specific team, or just events in a specific area. Like eBay, the site assumes no responsibility for your transaction—you deal only with the person you are buying from.

extreme sports

EXPN www.expn.go.com ⓒ ⓓ
Does "extreme leisure" sound like an oxymoron to you? Check out the Life & Styles section of EXPN, where coverage of the punk group Bad Religion is mixed with the skinny on the X Games, the big competition for skate, surf, and snowboarders. Click around this site to learn how to execute a backside fahrvergnugen or vote on who should replace Slater if he were to leave the Surfers. Pop-up menus and a Flash intro make this site chock-full of dazzle, but beware of broken links and a sometimes-buggy interface.

Adventure Sports Online www.adventuresports.com
Adventure Sports Online connects users to tour companies that offer the trekking, tubing, or llama travel they're looking for. But while the directory of guides and outfitters is the site's primary focus, users aren't sent downriver uninformed. Click on any of the varied sports and a host of training tips, publications, and gear recommendations appears. The only content-weak portion of this site is the TrailTalk forum—the last response we saw was months old.

EarthSports.com www.earthsports.com ⓓ
Woe unto all without Flash capabilities. If you don't have the plug-in, you'll miss the cool graphics and adrenaline-pumping music on this action sports site. Glitter aside, EarthSports.com does a mean job of covering surf, skate, snow, wake, and anything else that gets your heart racing, though, admittedly, its primary goal is to siphon your credit card number from your wallet. Just rationalize it this way: every time you purchase boots, boards, or bikinis here, you can collect Beenz to cash in for more awesome gear and even CDs.

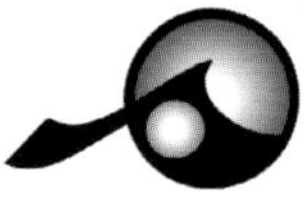

blue www.blueadventure.com

The adventure lifestyle, as defined by blue, involves exotic travel, eclectic music, and the latest gadgetry. You'll find separate sections for each on this flashy e-zine, as well as book reviews, travel guides, and trip recommendations. The site is geared toward the more discerning thrill-seeker, but some features are universally helpful—don't miss Urban Access, a cool interactive map that points out exciting experiences to be had within hours of New York, San Francisco, and L. A. (more cities to come).

Skateboarding.com www.skateboarding.com

Grind, slide and ollie your way through the slick online version of *Transworld Skateboarding Magazine*. No flashy intro here: this site gets right down to business, walking you through the basics of buying the right board, then teaching you how to master advanced tricks like the mamajama flip. The site also has extensive listings of skate parks across the nation and into Canada; choose a state, and the site provides information on the cost, terrain, and directions to each.

adrenalin-hit www.adrenalin-hit.com

The British reputation for prissiness gets a smack in the mouth at adrenalin-hit, a British e-zine that injects a generous dose of Flash and audio into its coverage of the adventure lifestyle. To see the features on snowboarding, skiing, and surfing, you'll want to head to the Riding section. When we checked, the eclectic articles there include first-person narratives, illustrated board-care demos, and a rant by Surfers Against Sewage. Navigating the site can seem like an extreme sport in itself, but a site map offers ever-ready help.

PlanetGirl's Indygirl www.indygirl.com

It's often forgotten that extreme sports are about adrenaline, not testosterone. Indygirl strikes back at the boys' club with a site dedicated to teen girls who live for sporting thrills. Big-name competitors take center stage, while visitors can get their time in the spotlight with user-submitted stories and profiles. It's about culture as much as sport; fashion and music features share billing with surf guides. Registration, though free, is required to explore, but also gets you members-only perks like newsletters and contests.

Skateboard.com www.skateboard.com

Skateboarders unite! Become a member of Skateboard.com's online haven for skaters and you'll receive free skateboard decals, a weekly newsletter, an email account, and special members-only content. You'll also find 29 essential maneuvers to becoming a great skateboarder (in Trick Tips), news on the latest skating products, skateboard assembly and safety (in the Resource Center), and enough contests to keep you busy seven days a week.

skyXtreme www.skyxtreme.com
If you aren't deterred by the site's Safety Issues section (which is practically a list of 101 ways to bounce), you'll find this homegrown e-zine bursting with features for the skydiving community. The homepage offers articles and news on innovative divers and dive centers, with an extensive list of competitions and meets around the world. Do you have your own story to tell? Send it in to Your Stories and see if you make the cut.

lifelounge.com www.lifelounge.com
If you can surf through the jam-packed layout, lifelounge.com sports the latest news and features on skate, snow, surf, inline, and bike sports. For each category, there's a photo gallery, industry news, product reviews, and profiles of the biggest players. How-tos guide you through building ramps and finding a prime surfing location, while the sections on fashion, music, and videogames offer a slice of board, blade, and bike culture.

Triathlete Magazine www.triathletemag.com
A site dedicated to both men and women of steel, this site doles out advice to anyone serious about strenuous athletic training. While it doesn't proffer the articles from this month's issue of the paper magazine, it's chock-full of information of its own on nutrition, supplements, and conditioning. If you need inspiration for your own training, or simply admire the human form, download some of the amazing shots of athletes.

Freebord www.freebord.com
Sporting some of the best graphics and video around, Freebord is really one big advertisement for a skateboard shaped like a snowboard, designed to execute on asphalt the heart-stopping slides and flips you see on the slopes. The demonstration videos here will give you newfound respect for the death-defying practitioners of this sport.

Climbing Magazine www.climbing.com
Climbing allows no room for error, and the editors of Climbing Magazine take their responsibilities very seriously indeed. The site offers extensive and authoritative articles on rock, ice, and sport climbing from the magazine's archive of past issues (though only summaries are given of current content). For personal and highly invigorating stories from the edge, see the Hot Flashes section. To create some stories of your own, start at the climbing sites and tours guide.

Board Universe www.boarduniverse.com
To the untrained eye, the boards used for surfing, skating, windsurfing, kitesurfing, and wakeboarding can look a lot alike. But practiced boarders should have no trouble picking their sport's board out of the pictures here, which allow access to QuickTime trick videos, news, equipment guides, and chat. The skate parks and beach reports are slanted toward Britain (the site's base).

Rocklist.com www.rocklist.com

Worth a site in and of itself, Rocklist.com's DataGuide is a growing database of the best scalable surfaces around the world. It's built on contributions from the climbing community—you too can add a listing and view detailed text descriptions, photos, and maps. Rocklist.com also features a half-dozen new articles each month (with a complete archive), as well as a Learn the Ropes educational center that hands out climbing tips like how to block a knot and the best gear for women climbers.

Dropzone.com www.dropzone.com

An online community for people united by a shared passion for falling out of the sky. Dropzone.com has a fairly equal mix of features on both the cultural side of skydiving and the sport's more technical aspects. The first is tended to by databases of both individual divers and drop zones across the globe, while the extensive Safety and Training section covers the latter. Newbies wanting to get off the ground would do well to check out the gear reviews.

TransWorld SURF www.transworldsurf.com

How's the surf? Find out at TransWorld SURF, proof that wave riders aren't just beach bums. Everything's here, from chat, classified ads, and business directories to webcam-based "surf checks" and step-by-step trick tips to get you grinding the curl with the best of them. Just like real surfing, however, the site is as much about the culture as the waves, so expect cultural bits like musician profiles and plenty of tongue-in-cheek humor.

windsurfer.com
www.windsurfer.com ©

Want to know if the surf's up in Aruba right this very minute? windsurfer.com puts you on top of the waves with real-time wind updates for anywhere the sea and air meet, as well as travel reviews, comparative board ratings, beginner tips, competition info, and an equipment shop to browse. Check out the Calculator, which tells you what the land, sea, and coastline conditions feel like at given wind speeds.

bluetorch.com www.bluetorch.com © ⓓ

bluetorch.com is dedicated to delivering hard-core commentary on surfing, wakeboarding, skating, and other extreme endeavors straight into the browsers of the devoted. Daily live webcasts and a staggering assortment of QuickTime video clips accompany the cool columns and feature articles. Read about a winning run at Pipeline or watch a clip of it happening. Then, get inside the athletes' heads—when they're not contributing first-person accounts, they're answering questions in the Profiles section.

Surfline www.surfline.com

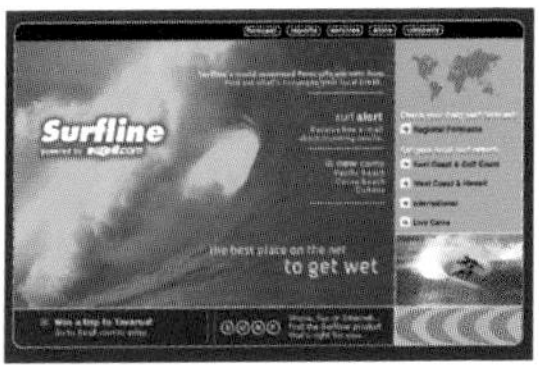

Your board, your shorts, and the weather report—surfing's three essentials. Surfline offers some of the most comprehensive beach weather and surf reports available on the Internet. Use the clickable map to check out the conditions on both coasts or view live streaming video feeds from around the world, including Baja, the Caribbean, Brazil, and Costa Rica. The site also offers several forecast delivery services, but keep in mind that access to the "toll-free" number actually costs $10.

fantasy sports

SmallWorld.com www.smallworld.com ⓞ

Like a farm league for fantasy sports players, SmallWorld.com lets its members perfect their technique before playing against more seasoned fantasy leaguers. The site tour familiarizes new users with the features of the site, How to Play teaches them the basics of being in a hockey, football, baseball, golf, or basketball league, and the Rules and FAQ answer specific questions. If you'd like to try it, sign up to be notified when registration opens for your favorite sport.

RotoNewsDirect www.rotonews.com

If there was ever an argument for substance over style, this is it. This site's straightforward interface and approach may pale against flashier competition, but you'd be hard pressed to find a more comprehensive fantasy sports site—there's enough news on hockey, racing, baseball, football, basketball, and golf to make you the most informed player in the site's free or pay leagues. Personalize the news page or have the info sent to your cell phone.

Prime Sports Interactive www.primesports.net

If there were a prize for best-integrated fantasy sportsite, Prime Sports Interactive might just be the winner. Its specialty is the development and hosting of fantasy leagues in football, baseball, hockey, golf, basketball and racing, both by computer and over the telephone. A smattering of news is presented, plenty of free games are offered, and cash prizes abound.

Rotisserie League Baseball Association www.usastats.com

Before it was called "fantasy sports," it was the "rotisserie leagues." This association is the authority on the original brand of fantasy baseball (and now, basketball), making it the best place to set up a league and track statistics. They'll even give you expert advice on running a standard or custom league. Quality costs, however—be prepared to pay at least $40 per team to get started.

Fanball www.fanball.com
Want a side order of sports news with that fantasy league play? Go to Fanball, where news, scores, and lively features support a system of stat-based games and contests. Straightforward fantasy football, baseball, and golf leagues are the main attraction, but there are also more specific competitions like the $10,000 Home Run Challenge.

Virtual Racing www.vrace.com ©
Auto racing may not be the highest-profile fantasy sport, but you wouldn't know that after visiting Virtual Racing. Every type of circuit imaginable is covered, with driver profiles, team packages, track histories, status reports, technical information (down to the chassis and tires), and anything else you'll need to take the checkered flag. You'll find an exhaustive amount of data, but it's easily navigable so finding the pole position isn't a chore.

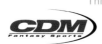

CDM Fantasy Sports www.cdmnet.com
This site is ground zero for fantasy sports, with big games, big contests, and even bigger cash prizes (try $25,000). Choose from a variety of games in five sports (baseball, football, hockey, basketball, and golf); the price of joining ranges from free to $50. If you want endorsements, know that *USA Today*, MSNBC, golf.com, and The Hockey News all run their leagues through CDM.

FantasyTeam Sports www.fantasyteam.com
There are lots of fantasy gaming sites, but FantasyTeam Sports differentiates itself with one key quality: variety. Where else are you going to find active leagues in ATP tennis, F1 racing, and cricket? The usual suspects (baseball) are here, too, for a total of nine sports covered. News, scores, and special reports help round out the package for the armchair coach.

Fantasy Insights www.fantasyinsights.com ©

Its name may be suggestive, but the most enticing thing about Fantasy Insights is its potential for aiding in your fantasy league success. Primarily geared toward football (with a complementary baseball component), this site provides articles, charts, news, and analysis specifically put together for fantasy gaming. You can order one of the premium packages for neatly compiled information delivered to you at various stages of the season, but there's plenty of analysis to be had for the low, low price of free.

Sandbox.com www.sandbox.com

In fantasy sports, the winning and losing may be virtual but the gloating is very real. Sandbox.com is one of the more popular places to join a fantasy league—the site offers baseball, football, hockey, motor sports, and golf, and a business league that follows the stock market. To keep you on top of your team's standing, there's tons of news and in-depth analysis; point your rival toward the Casino for arcade games to distract him from his stats.

SportsRocket.com www.sportsrocket.com

Sports fans and gamers can combine their passions on SportsRocket.com. Play online games (some are Shockwave) of auto racing, baseball, golf, and soccer, or try your luck at one of the many contests or trivia challenges. If you're the best in the field, you can win prizes like a free CD or $3,000. And if you've always wanted to get your hands on your favorite hockey player's old jersey, bring your winnings to the auction block where you can barter for sports cards, gear, and other memorabilia.

Fantasy Sports Advice www.fantasysportsadvice.com

The name says it all. This site is destined to become every fantasy gaming fanatic's best friend, on the ready with an endless number of useful tips and statistics to help you stay on top of every step of the season. The scope of the site is limited to major sports—focusing on football, baseball, and basketball—but that focus affords in-depth coverage both in season and out. Paying subscribers get customized email advice, draft packages, and premium scouting info dropped on their Internet doorstep, but the free goodies are bountiful as well.

SportsLine Commissioner www.commissioner.com

SportsLine Commissioner is high-powered fantasy sports management software that lets you run your own sports league. The advantage? Simply more frills and features than most free sites offer. The Commissioner lets users customize rules and scoring, and enjoy live updates on a personalized Web page. Some software is free, others offer a free 14-day trial period and a fee after that.

Fitness Online www.fitnessonline.com

While dishing out tailor-made health, fitness, and nutrition advice, Fitness Online isn't afraid to admit that steaming things up in the bedroom can be one of the best exercises around. Intrigued? Then click over to the site to read through more unconventional fitness tips, or catch up on the latest urban diet fads, day spas, and (serious) exercise regimes. The site is one of few that gives excellent fitness information without being overly commercial.

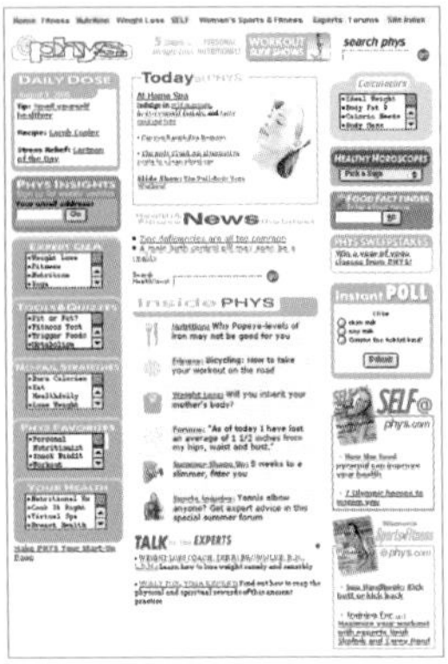

Phys.com www.phys.com

Phys.com is physical fitness for women that covers the gamut from weight loss to nutrition and exercise. Lots of advice here on eating healthfully and sculpting your bod into bikini-worthy perfection (whatever happened to being active for fun?). Skip the Snack Bandit virtual slot machine and go straight to the Nutritional Rx page for sound advice on how to prevent illness. Cool calculators let you figure out your ideal body weight, body fat percentage (yikes), or daily carbohydrate needs in a couple clicks of the mouse.

The Yoga Site www.yogasite.com

The Yoga Site seeks to promote fitness, flexibility, and stress relief through this time-honored discipline. Practically all of your questions about yoga will be answered on the FAQ page, and those that aren't can be submitted via email. Seasoned practitioners and novices alike will appreciate the teacher directory, style guide, and organization listings. A retreat directory is also here.

Thriveonline www.thriveonline.com

A very cool site dedicated to personal health and happiness, Thriveonline contains a host of ideas and advice in areas such as fitness, sexuality, and serenity to improve physical and emotional wellness. Each area includes self-assessment quizzes complete with advice and explanations of the results, experts to answer questions, boards and chat, news, tips, and more. From recipes to exercise programs to tantric sex instruction, Thriveonline is a complete wellness source.

BigFitness.com www.bigfitness.com

Exercise your clicking finger by picking out stationary bikes, dumbbell racks, pulse monitors, and fat analyzers at BigFitness.com. You may get a workout sifting through the site's low-tech interface, but not enough to break a sweat. Click through to the Reebok Store for sleek elliptical trainers and treadmills—and throw away that candy bar!

Workout Warehouse www.workoutwarehouse.com
You don't need to spend a lot of money to get in shape, as evidenced by the Workout Warehouse Web site. It's got home fitness equipment at deep discounts right from the manufacturer. Whether you're in the market for a NordicTrack skier, a Pro-Form treadmill, or an Image stationary bike, you're bound to find a bargain. Check out the installment payment plans if you're buying a big-ticket item.

Asimba www.asimba.com
For those who can't afford the steep cost of a personal trainer or weight loss center, Asimba is a godsend. The site helps you create custom fitness and diet programs for any level, whether you want to train for a marathon or just a jog around the block. A few of these plans will cost you, but there's a ton of help to be had for free, including a log to keep track of daily eating and exercise and the option to have it all emailed to your computer or downloaded to your Palm Pilot.

Prevention.com www.prevention.com
How best to lose weight and keep it lost? What's a healthy finger food? Women.com has taken *Prevention* magazine under its wing and produced an online version that answers questions on women's health and fitness, with a particular emphasis on diet and nutrition. Cool interactive tools like a virtual spa and vitamin quiz make up for the fact that some of the articles are only teasers for those in the print version.

MuscleMaster.com www.musclemaster.com

Guns, pipes, bazookas—whatever you call those bulging beauties known as your biceps, doubtless this online supplement megastore has something for them. The stock includes everything from Pro-hGH (a "natural growth hormone") to ginseng to chocolate cheesecake protein bars, and shipping is free for orders of more than $100. In addition to shopping, the surprisingly well-versed site also has numerous articles on slimming down, bulking up, and getting fit (with suggestions of helpful products, of course).

YogaDirectory.com www.yogadirectory.com
Meditate on this: YogaDirectory.com has almost 1,000 links to everything yoga. Though the site's strength doesn't lie in feature content (the only original material comes in the form of personals and discussion boards), it can direct you to other sites with details on different yoga traditions, the history of the practice, and instructional products for sale. A good place to know about in an area that lacks a comprehensive hub.

BodyTrends.com www.bodytrends.com
In a market dominated by treadmill peddlers and Stairmaster e-tailers, BodyTrends.com is a refreshing alternative. The site offers less common exercise equipment like yoga mats, water weights, medicine balls, and boxing gloves along with larger cardio machines. Articles on fitness and health ("How to Choose a Health Club", "Fitness Fiction") culled from assorted sources help make up for an as-seen-on-TV undertone and occasionally clunky interface.

TrainingforSport.com www.trainingforsport.com

Truly dedicated athletes take exhaustion as a sign that the hard part of their workout has just begun. It is this group of athletes that TrainingforSport.com serves. The site uses data from four drills (like the standing long jump) to form a picture of an athlete's current fitness level and then recommends exercises, nutrition, and rest that will improve his or her performance in a specific sport. This is no weight-loss, bun-toning regime—these people are aiming for raw power and speed.

eFit www.efit.com ©

If simply reading health information could get you fit, then eFit has the content to turn you into the next Arnold Schwarzenegger. Constantly updated, in-depth articles accompany comprehensive evaluations of different exercise regimes to guide you towards health, strength, and desired weight. eFit will even get personal and tailor an exercise or diet plan for you, right down to the restaurants in your neighborhood.

gymamerica.com www.gymamerica.com ⓓ

Weight machines and cardio equipment can be daunting for gym newbies, and consultation is always expensive. Here's an alternative. In eight simple steps, this site assesses your fitness goals and creates a workout designed specifically to address them. There are even animated diagrams of specific exercises such as flyes and dips, providing a definitive answer to questions about correct technique. Additional articles on health, nutrition, and even a healthy sex life round out the site.

FitForAll www.fitforall.com ©

FitForAll promises total well-being in four simple steps: learn it, do it, talk about it, and shop for it. To that end, the site provides reading material by M.D.s on a variety of basic topics, a selection of pre-fab exercise plans, a message board accessible even to non-members, and an online storefront. For that health club feel, a pending exclusive membership option will also get you one-on-one coaching and other personalized help.

Health and Fitness Online www.healthandfitness.com

Did you know chicken soup is a great post-workout food? You will after visiting Health and Fitness Online. Insightful fitness-related advice is plentiful here, but the best resources are the trainer and gym searches, offering simple hunts via zip code. The site is still gearing up, so news archives don't reach back terribly far, but then again there is the gawk-worthy fitness model gallery...

InfoSlim www.infoslim.com

The pickings at InfoSlim are anything but, with plenty of advice on nutrition, exercise, and stress reduction from health experts. A lot of sites claim "expert advice," so the actual resumes of the M.D.s and R.N.s on staff here are a good sign. Custom-crafted workouts and diets come with membership (and its monthly fee), but tabs at the top of the homepage are the gateway to free information on all aspects of health.

Fitness Find www.fitnessfind.com

If you want an exercise in frustration, try finding the answer to a specific health question on the Internet without sifting through hundreds of links. Fitness Find simplifies the process by doing the legwork for you. Here, you'll find scores of articles collected from sites like GORP and Thriveonline.com, arranged in easy categories like Weight Training, Injury, and Fitness and Food. While the site could be more comprehensive (and the homepage less cluttered with ads), what's here works well.

football

Players Inc. www.nflplayers.com

Dedicated to "taking the helmets off the players," Players Inc. lets you in on the personal lives of the pros. Mine the profiles of a ton of big name stars for the scoop on their childhoods, hobbies, and eccentric interests; where else can you find out that Atlanta Falcon Terance Mathis once considered quitting football to work on his basketball skills? Even lesser sports celebs get the treatment, with special sections like Rookie Premiere and Unsung Heroes of the NFL.

NFL.com www.nfl.com

NFL.com breaks down the professional football season week by week so you can relish each and every step of the climb to the Super Bowl. Fans can also get info on how to buy tickets to upcoming games, brush up on team stats, look over the career highlights of favorite players, and drop in on the Coaches Club page. There's even a kids page for pint-sized pigskin enthusiasts.

NFL Shop www.nflshop.com

Armchair quarterbacks rejoice! Be a part of the gridiron action with official NFL Shop essentials, like the inflatable Chicago Bears chair or the personalized Dallas Cowboys jersey. There are even tie-dyed team T-shirts for the hippie sports fan up the street (not that you'd ever hang out with him, but still).

FootballBoards.com www.footballboards.com

FootballBoards.com is a community site for pigskin fans that is made up solely of message boards where fans can post opinions on topics like "Who is the greatest coach of all time?" or the dubiously sports-related "What are your favorite movies?", with the more general topics getting the most traffic. Postings in each usually stick to the topic at hand, as a site staffer moderates every one.

NFL Europe www.nfleurope.com

Thunder, Fire, Dragons, Galaxy—they may sound like the ingredients for a fantasy novel, but globally minded sports buffs know them as four of Europe's "American football" teams. This up-and-coming (in Europe) sport has its online home here, with thorough news, history, and a multimedia section for each of the teams. A handy (if temperamental) translation link is provided for the feature articles, which are each written in their team's native tongue.

NFLfans.com www.nflfans.com ©

Perhaps you prefer news that's "by the fans, for the fans," rather than information that's been funneled through the mouthy media. This site offers a direct line to the info that NFL followers really want—rookie previews, scouting videos, animated game highlights—as well as access to the NFL Vault and links to fantasy sites. Sign up for the NFL Messenger to receive weekly news emails fresh off the wire; we guarantee you won't miss one second of the entire football season.

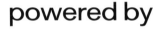

arenafootball2 www.af2.com

Arena football became an official league sport in 1987. But only recently has it become popular as something of a farm league for the NFL—many professional players got their start in the AFL, including Kurt Warner. This site is dedicated to stats and news on the league, with a specific page devoted to each of the fifteen teams. Some sections of the recently launched site are still growing, so you'll have to check back to see how the news archive and children's section fill out.

Pro Football Hall of Fame www.profootballhof.com

You won't get to rub the big, bronze bust of Joe Montana, but in most other ways a virtual visit to the Pro Football Hall of Fame measures up to a real one. Peruse bios, news, and history, or get the latest updates on modern day sports heroes—those already immortalized and those soon-to-be. User polls take surfers' suggestions on daily topics like the best linebackers in history or various criteria for entry to the Hall.

ArenaFan Online www.arenafan.net

ArenaFan Online promotes that 50-yard indoor war known as arena football. The site's fast pace and overall intensity threatens to upstage pages devoted to its outdoor counterpart. In fact, the main page verges on manic; if you have a favorite team, you might want to click on its logo at the top of the homepage to go straight to its subsection. Registered members get access to the site's free fantasy leagues, chat rooms, and polls.

football.com www.football.com ©

If football.com's writers seem to live and breathe the sport, it's because they do—they're football players. The site gets much of its news and feature content straight from the guys who make it. Doug O'Brian, kicker for the New Orleans Saints, contributes to three different columns, including a daily diary of his life on and off the field. There are also three separate forums for querying an agent, a player, and a coach, if you manage to invent a question that isn't answered in the excruciating amount of information here.

Monday Night Online www.abcmnf.go.com

Are you ready for some football? ABC's Monday Night Football Web site has more than just the game schedule and football news—most notably, a Sight & Sound multimedia area, where fans can view weekly highlights, tune into audio commentary, or flip through still shots of gridiron greats. The site also sports MNF's own fantasy league, discussion and chat forums, and (get this) four different versions of Hank Williams Jr.'s classic theme song.

Pro Football Weekly www.profootballweekly.com

Too embarrassed to ask your buddies at the Super Bowl party what a "nickel and dime" defense is? Check out Pro Football Weekly's Football 101 lessons, which break down new topics like "The 3-4 vs. the 4-3 Defense" each and every week. Adapted from the print edition, Pro Football Weekly is also a great site for fantasy league play and engaging editorials from head-honcho Ron Pollack.

Maxfootball.com www.maxfootball.com

With personalized audio and video programming at its core, the Max offers fans with broadband some of the latest in interactive sporting news. The site's field correspondents call in daily and provide a first-person perspective on games, while the video section has team-by-team commentary from Jerry Glanville and Gary Horton. Of course, you can also drool over the latest news, scores and statistics, share your gripes with fellow fans, or purchase team gear all with a few clicks.

AllMadden.com www.foxsports.com/allmadden ⓞ

All Madden, all the time. Whether you love him or hate him, you can't escape him—Madden has become such a well-loved analyst for the FOX network, they gave him his own Web site. Check out this fun and simply designed site to find out who makes the All Madden teams and which games are his picks of the week. Finally, you need no longer be in San Francisco to get your dose of John each weekday morning.

NFL High School Football www.nflhs.com ©

A site that finally gives the crown jewel of high school athletics its due, NFL High School Football brings together first-rate advice for coaches, players, and officials. Currently, the Coaches Corner is the most developed area. Or, click on your state on the national map for news of recent games, players to watch, and links to sites of local interest. Cool extras like training tips and an interactive playbook are peppered throughout.

Superbowl.com www.superbowl.com ⓞ

If you missed the Superbowl this past January and suddenly get curious in August, this is the place to go. Stuffed with slide shows, post-game interviews, and interactive playbooks, Superbowl.com brings the game right to your computer, regardless of month. Arguably more fun though, are the tips on throwing a really great Super Bowl party. #1: Put a television in the bathroom so that no one misses any of the action or commercials.

Superbowl-Ads.com www.superbowl-ads.com ⓞ

Arguably the only instance where the commercials draw as many viewers as the show, Super Bowl ads get cataloged in all their high-tech, high-priced glory on this site. Remember the Bud Wassup? How about that Pets.com one? You can view any of them in QuickTime format—all commercials are between two and six megabytes, so they download fairly fast. After you've seen them all, vote for your favorites and/or read about the hype.

SBC Cotton Bowl www.swbellcottonbowl.com ©

Everything you wanted to know about the Cotton Bowl is here, from ticketing info to a history of the 64-year-old game. Scour stadium seating charts before getting tickets, brush up on bowl trivia, or peruse the video vault. Our favorite feature, the Cotton Bowl Hall of Fame, gives a brief history and lets you look for your favorite players by inaugural year and era.

Orange Bowl Festival www.orangebowl.org

The first wire photo transmitted by the Associated Press was from the first Orange Bowl in Miami in 1935. Bucknell beat Miami 26-0 in that classic game and in the years since, dozens of different schools have been involved in the Orange Bowl. This site has the history and highlights from all of them, as well as a ton of helpful information if you plan to attend this year's game—a schedule for the parade, tailgating party information, Orange Bowl merchandise, and a link for tickets.

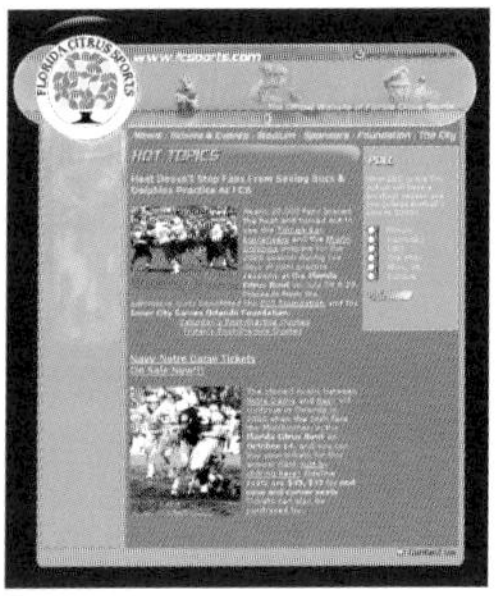

Florida Citrus Sports www.fcsports.com
Though the splash page looks like an orange juice ad, this site is actually chock full of Florida football coverage. Choosing breadth over depth, Florida Citrus Sports sets ticket information for the annual Women's Football Clinic next to shots of the Miami Dolphins. And of course, they provide extensive coverage on the Florida Citrus Bowl, including everything from seating charts to the location of ATMs inside the stadium.

St. Louis Rams www.stlouisrams.com
Kurt Warner's amazing sob story of working as a supermarket stock boy the year before leading the Rams to win Superbowl XXXIV is nowhere to be found here. Instead, for a refreshing change, the site focuses on the entire team with news, stats, and a new in-depth feature article every couple of weeks. There is also a shop for merchandise, and ticketing information with a clickable stadium that lets you see the view from any seat (though you'll have to call to actually buy a ticket).

MiamiDolphins.com www.miamidolphins.com
Not the most hardcore of the official NFL team sites (the first link on the main page sends you to the Dolphins' cheerleaders), but definitely a fun and interactive way to explore the famed Miami team. Along with a Press Box full of team news, the site hosts a virtual tour of training camp, more individual player stats than even the biggest Dol-fan could swallow, and Q & A with the pros (though it seems they only answer questions during the season).

gambling

World Wide Tele Sports www.betwwts.com
Don't judge a booking site by its cover—this haven for the sports numbers enthusiast may not win any awards for design, but it's overflowing with informative features. Keep track of lines and scores in real-time and register for membership to lay down your bets. You might not be able to find out what your favorite players had for breakfast the morning of the game, but they get you about as close as you'll ever get.

Daily Racing Form www.drf.com ©

The early bird gets the best betting info at Daily Racing Form, a century-old print publication-turned-Web site that updates its track information at 7 a.m. each morning. You'll find entries on every track in North America and England—with race results available 30 minutes after each race ends—and helpful handicapping tools. Getting the full features requires a subscription (upwards of $60/month), but the news, race talk audio links, and results are among the free features.

The Sands of the Caribbean Online Casino www.thesands.com

Act like a Las Vegas high roller from the comfort of your home. This online casino is perhaps the most reputable on the Web (and they have the stats to prove it) and offers free software that enables users to link up to a network of online gamblers—including a hefty population of sports bettors. Download the program, practice offline, make a deposit, and then pick from a number of games based on hockey, horse racing, football, and more.

flutter.com www.flutter.com

Gambling is big business, but the most fun wagers are made between coworkers, friends, and denizens of the local sports bar. flutter.com makes this kind of competition easier by providing a forum where enterprising users can propose and accept sports bets, setting the stakes and odds themselves. Though the site emphasizes games in Europe and quotes prices in British pounds, special sections are set aside for American sports. Take the tour to learn the ropes, and then try your luck.

07 Sports Betting www.07sportsbetting.com

07 Sports Betting makes risking money on the athletic performance of others easier than ever, with a straightforward interface and easy-to-use registration process. You'll find a bountiful selection of sports with a focus on American and British favorites. There's also an online casino and a Play-for-Fun option for those too young or too cautious to put real money on the line.

Vegas Insider.com www.vegasinsider.com ⓒ ⓞ

Rounders can't beat the odds on this site with picks straight from Sin City. This informative online newsletter contains everything a serious gambler needs to make betting a simple matter. From the real-time odds ticker, clear and concise format with rankings, odds, picks, and sport news, one has to wonder why they even bother with the tips and handicapping tools. Whether it's basketball or football, collegiate or professional, this site helps bettors hedge their bets.

golf

PGATour.com www.pgatour.com

Can't get enough of Tiger Woods and his winning ways? Then log onto PGATour.com, where you'll find articles on the Michael Jordan of golf, as well as tour news, video highlights, and Q & As with the pros. Still trying to master your own chip shot? Read the Life on Tour first-person essays for some inspiration, then head to the site's practice tee for a strategy session.

Tiger Woods www.tigerwoods.com

You've seen him on dozens of magazine covers and, of course, on TV, so it's no surprise that the hottest player on the PGA tour has his very own Web site. Log on here to learn hows, wheres, and whys of Tiger: his career earnings ($19,007,950 at press time), his driver (a Titleist Titanium 975D), and the time he putted with Bob Hope at age two. Most worthy features: audio and video links, and scheduled chat with the legend himself.

GOLFonline www.golfonline.com ⓒ ⓓ

If spending hours on the courses isn't enough for you, then head to GOLFonline—the site is (perhaps too) crowded with news headlines on the major tours, information on courses and equipment, and tips to improve your game. The coolest part? GOLFonline's instructional videos, which let you watch mini-QuickTime movies of top golfers explaining their techniques.

GOLF Magazine's Golf Course Guide www.golfcourse.com ⓞ

Finding a great course is fifty percent of any successful golf outing, which makes this online "link to the links" essential for both amateur and serious duffers. Over 2,000 courses in the U.S. and abroad can be located through a comprehensive, easy-to-use search engine or by reading original "best of" lists like "100 best modern courses." We'll forgive their use of the magazine's archives to feed the site (some content dates to 1998), but we could go without the pop-up ads.

Shark.com www.shark.com
"Attack life" is the motto of this golf magazine-cum-lifestyle site brought to you by renowned golfer Greg "The Shark" Norman. While the content is worthwhile, the coverage is a bit unwieldy, treating everything from custom-fitted clubs to health controversies, travel ideas, and of course, golfing tips. We had to go to the FAQ to understand just what the site was up to, but once you figure it out, there's some interesting information on offer.

golf.com www.golf.com ©
The complete coverage of the NBC network with the additional news and streaming audio one can only get from the Web. golf.com has absolutely everything a golf enthusiast might want to know from tournament news and statistics to the latest in high tech grips and shafts. But the site is not just for the seasoned professional—it also offers expert advice on gear and equipment and links that show you where to find lessons and golf-oriented travel for the family.

Golf Club Exchange.com www.golfclubexchange.com
Find equipment and embrace your competitive side with Golf Club Exchange.com, an online auction house specializing in used clubs. It's a person-to-person deal, with the site acting as the middleman to make sure both parties are satisfied. Sellers must agree to guaranteed shipment and a 48-hour purchase evaluation period before payment becomes final. Buyers, in turn, are bound to pay on completed transactions. If you don't see the clubs you're looking for, register with the ClubFinder and the site will email you if they show up within the next eight weeks.

TheGolfChannel.com www.thegolfchannel.com ©
On television, the Golf Channel is home to golf coverage 24 hours a day, so you'd be right to expect its Web presence to be comprehensive. With plenty of news and analysis on every golf tour, live tournament coverage, and insightful columns, you're never out-of-the-know. You can also get a few of the television programs—including *Golf Central, Viewer's Forum,* and *Academy Live*—on demand if you have the Windows Media Player. Almost better than cable.

Golfweek.com www.golfweek.com
A rare feather-filled golf ball recently sold at Christie's for a record price of $42,600, reports Golfweek.com's Forecaddie. The columnist, just one of the site's 10, offers new revelations each week that add color to a fairly standard assortment of pro, college, and amateur golf news. You'll also want to visit here to take advantage of the News Ranger, a service that sends readers an email to alert them of articles that correspond to the interests they have entered.

Golfsearch.com www.golfsearch.com ©

Finding a great golf site among the chaff on the Net can be harder than finding a ball in the rough, but Golfsearch.com makes it easier with a thorough exploration of golf content in cyberspace. Sites are slotted into a wide range of categories from Fun & Humor (if you're looking for a great golf joke), to Retail (for discount merchandise and golf art), and Real Estate (golf-home buying guides) making navigation a snap. But if clicking is too much, save yourself the time and try Golfsearch.com's own search engine.

Taylor Made www.taylormadegolf.com

Taylor Made is the company that brought metal-headed woods to the golf course, and now they bring them to the Internet in a very comprehensive electronic storefront. The cool design, zoomable pictures, and extensive descriptions make it simple for users to decide which irons, woods, putters, or rescue clubs they need. You won't be able to buy clubs online, but the company has provided schedules for product demos and clinics, and a great dealer locator to steer you to a brick-and-mortar store.

The Masters www.masters.org ©

If there's one golf tournament familiar to even non-fans, it's the Masters at Augusta National. Activity at the event's Web home is hottest during actual play, but there's enough history, statistics, and multimedia to make it worthwhile year-round. Get profiles on the participants or commentary from golf legend Jack Nicklaus (who knows a thing or two about the winner's green jacket). Particularly cool are the live webcams and remote cameras that allow you to get a customizable view of this venerable course.

MyGolf.com www.mygolf.com ©

An e-commerce storefront for highbrow and grassroots golfers alike. Brand loyalists will appreciate being able to click on their logo of choice to go directly to the stock by that company, while shoppers who don't need the latest and greatest will benefit from a quick trip through the site's equipment auction. Navigation is concise and logical throughout, and a thorough customer service policy assures satisfaction (though if you return an item after 30 days or in "non-new" condition they'll charge you 25% of the purchase price).

LPGA.com www.lpga.com ©

The LPGA has just turned 50, and by the looks of it, every bit of information from that half-century has been packed into the association's site. Live webcasts and leaderboards of current tournaments, a history of past ones, player profiles, and instructional animations are all here. We suggest heading to the site map (a link is located on the upper right corner) before you're overpowered by the homepage.

GolfReview.com
www.golfreview.com

Get the skinny on the best and worst in golf equipment from the people who would know—your fellow golfers. User reviews are the focus of activity at GolfReview.com, where you can read visitor opinions on resort courses, clubs, golf shoes, and the always-sexy golf pants. Want to learn how to rust your new RTG sand wedge for maximum spin? Head to the message boards.

GolfServ www.golfserv.com

Who needs expensive lessons when GolfServ offers more than 250 mini-courses that instruct on topics like swing, sand play, and putting? The lessons themselves aren't high-tech by any means (think black-and-white illustrations), but they get the job done. While you're scouting for skills you can also find a course on which to practice, connect with other golfers in your city, and set and evaluate a handicap.

Nicklaus.com www.nicklaus.com

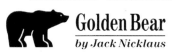

The Golden Bear's site is chock full of the kind of diverse golf know-how one could only accumulate during an extended career on the PGA and Senior tours. Aside from the expected pictures and golf tips, you can also read the Jack Nicklaus International Golf Club seasonal newsletter, get weekly commentary on Nicklaus' tour progress, and buy Golden Bear products. Navigation from one feature to the next—aided by handy pop-up menus—is as smooth as his swing.

teetimes.com www.teetimes.com

Reserve tee times online? Now that's technology. teetimes.com lets putters browse courses in 14 states and book a spot quickly and easily. Each course listing includes fees, discounts, dress code, and features (snack bar!), so you know before you go. Click on Free Golf to see a short list of courses where you can play free this week, or the travel page to book a golf vacation.

Chipshot.com www.chipshot.com

Imagine a department store where each department outfits a different type of golfer and you've got the concept behind Chipshot.com. There's merchandise and equipment here for players of all kinds, including a special section for lefties. If you need help choosing, the site lists the clubs that are selling the best, which experts use, and which are made specifically for men, women, and juniors. An extensive customer service section covers every possible service issue (some with video clips), and FedEx 3-day domestic shipping is free for every order.

BuyGolf.com www.buygolf.com

Don't fool yourself, kid; golf isn't just a game, it's an industry. A peek at this Web site makes it clear within the first few clicks. Hawking everything from day schools for beginners to personal driving ranges for zealots, BuyGolf.com has items for every member of the family, including experts and lefties. If you've got a set of clubs to spare, auction them off at the linked Golf Club Exchange page.

GolfsPast.com www.golfspast.com

GOLFSPAST.COM
The History of Golf

From the first Scotsman hitting balls in a field back in the 17th century to the bright lights of the PGA tour, this site encompasses golf's entire illustrious history. All sorts of features wax nostalgic on course architecture, great competitions of the past, and the historic personalities that made them happen. If memorabilia is your thing, you can both peruse (read letters between the old-time greats) and purchase.

Golfmonitor.com www.golfmonitor.com

A no-nonsense buying guide that compares competing products by price and quality, without a lot of marketing mumbo-jumbo. Come to Golfmonitor.com when you want to pit fairway woods against each other or get a coupon for Callaway balls from an online retailer like buy.com or gball.com. Much of the actual content (reviews, user opinions, etc.) is culled from other sites like epinions.com, but the service of compiling all this consumer information in one place is a worthy one.

Planet Golf www.planetgolf.com

Golf has a reputation for being somewhat stuffy, but Planet Golf gives that image a kick in the pants. Based in Venice, California, this site takes a laid-back approach to outfitting the golfer, adding goofy extras like four separate versions of the company's history and plenty of shameless celebrity-laden self-promotion to its selection of apparel. You should, however, be able to find clothing for even the most formal round through the fairly straightforward interface.

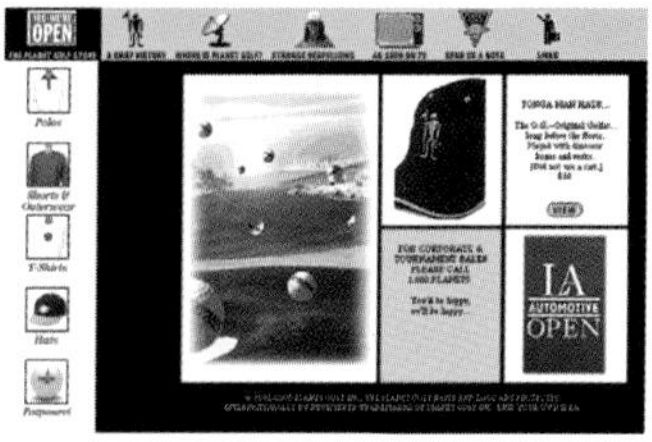

MyScorecard.com www.myscorecard.com

A handy, high-tech tool for formulating and tracking a handicap. Register at MyScorecard.com to calculate a handicap, keep track of your golf scores, and email them to friends directly. If you want to learn all the convoluted algorithms behind the handicap calculation, click into the Knowledge Center. On the other hand, you could just let the site do the work for you.

GolfDigest.com www.golfdigest.com

Casual golfers step aside—the online version of *Golf Digest* is for players who are serious about improving their game. Find tips from the Tiger on how to deal with your next short-side pitch (or your grouchy partner). Weekend warriors will appreciate the easy-to-surf navigation here; the site is organized into intuitive sections like How to Play, Where to Play, and What to Play, and offers complete tour coverage and other news.

Mr. Golf Etiquette www.mrgolf.com

Where should you place the pin when putting? What's the proper way to enter a bunker? If you don't know the answers, never fear. Mr. Golf, a self-styled guru of course etiquette, runs a site dedicated to making sporting gentlepersons of us all. However, learning these P's and Q's is more fun than just reading a page, thanks to a photo-driven Etiquette Game that teaches and tests at the same time.

drkoop.com www.drkoop.com ©

Suffering from fibromyalgia or minor, ahem, discomfort because of some particularly tight sporting gear? drkoop.com offers up smart information on these and more basic problems in its Conditions & Concerns section, helping you figure out what's going on with your body when something's not quite right. Other resources here, notably the medical encyclopedia and the health tool set, won't intimidate even the most doctor-phobic patient.

Men's Health www.menshealth.com

Are you building muscle or just wasting time? Can a simple aspirin really help heart disease? The short and informative articles at Men's Health Magazine's Web site have the answers, and the archive holds two years' worth of them. Searching through the past editions is free, though you'll have to pay to actually see the articles. Sign up for the weekly health and fitness newsletter for info without a price tag.

WebMD www.webmd.com

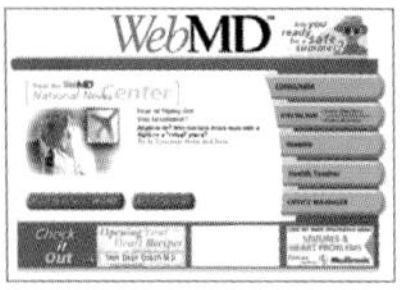

Tune in here to live, professionally facilitated conversations on topics like raising twins, or living with anorexia or arthritis. This eclectic mix of topics makes the Live Events Channel at WebMD worth visiting. But the site also offers a broad variety of health-related advice and practical services such as My Health Record, a place where families can safely and conveniently store their medical records online.

AllHerb.com www.allherb.com © ⓓ ⓢ

Why not try an all-natural cure for whatever ails you? AllHerb.com offers a wide range of herbal medicines, as well as simple info for people just looking to explore. Search by herb, vitamin, or supplement, or enter an ailment and the site will make a suggestion. The high-quality customer service here includes flat-fee shipping, no sales tax, and a personal health page.

HealthAtoZ.com www.healthAtoZ.com ©

Laid out like a virtual health club, HealthAtoZ.com's Fitness Center has distinct sections for information on weight training, aerobics, and "mind-body practices" (that's yoga to you and me). Each page covers topics that gym rats wonder about, like whether the calorie readout on the treadmill is accurate. The site even has a Juice Bar for chatting it up with fellow fitness freaks.

eNutrition www.enutrition.com

The name may be cyber-trendy but the contents of eNutrition are solid. Each of its five categories (Weight Management, Your Health, Sports Nutrition, Vitamins & More, Body & Senses) is backed up by a comprehensive group of products that will help you slim down, de-stress, or just get healthier. Breaking health news, gift baskets for fitness fanatics, and a glossary of terms from "absorption" to "yeast" round out the offerings. Shipping specials change weekly, so check back often.

eDiets.com www.ediets.com ⓞ

eDiets.com™

Personalized diets, fitness and counseling online

Don't know the difference between a crunch and a squat? Let the animated fitness instructor at eDiets.com show you exactly how to get the most out of your exercise routine. The licensed dieticians and counselors at eDiets.com will also supply you with weekly meal plans, shopping lists, and motivation specifically tailored to your personalized diet profile. But while the profile is free, the program is not—though eDiets.com claims that its approach costs about half as much as traditional diet programs.

AccentHealth.com www.accenthealth.com ©

Many health practitioners now encourage their patients to use both conventional and holistic practices, a combination known as complementary medicine. AccentHealth.com can help you seek out the best of both worlds by offering each side's info on everything from fixing a broken nose to managing weight. Use the search box to go straight to the topic that interests you. Athletes will also appreciate the Virtual Fitness Program, which pairs up users so they can monitor and motivate each other's progress.

CBSHealthWatch www.healthwatch.com ©

For those of us who can't remember when we last visited the doctor, CBSHealthWatch offers a unique tool called the Daily Diary that lets you track medication, doctor visits, diet, and exercise. But while the Daily Diary even allows users to graph their records, it doesn't come with clear written instructions; users may also get confused by the icons that look deceptively like links.

Netrition www.netrition.com

From low-carb pancake mix (it really exists!) to protein shakes and grape seed extract, Netrition.com is an online market for well-priced nutritional products. There are hundreds of foods, supplements, body building products, and nutrients available, and each listing includes a detailed description of the product with data such as calories, total fat, and protein. You'll find the newest products on the home page, and a huge list of the nutritional value of different foods in the Info section.

peakhealth.net www.peakhealth.net ©

Have a question or two about your optimal health? Click on peakhealth.net's Live button to interact with a real person or send an email to Ask Doctor for personalized advice. You can use the site to find and buy everything from energy bars and meal replacements to your everyday multi-vitamin. Once you've finished shopping, check out the features such as "Controlling carbohydrates with a low glycemic diet" or recommended spots for additional health research on the Web.

FoodFit.com www.foodfit.com ©

The closest thing to a personal chef you'll find on the Web, this site takes an interactive approach to healthy eating. Its tools section has weight and calorie calculators, a shopping checklist of pantry essentials, and a profile that helps pinpoint your dietary strengths and weaknesses. Register for membership, and your data will be there each time you return. The site is also stocked with recipes, kitchen tips, and feature articles on the newest non-fat foods.

HealthSCOUT www.healthscout.com

HealthSCOUT cuts through the clutter of health info by delivering news to athletes on only those topics that interest them, like women's health or alternative healing. Register with the site, pick your preferences, and it designs a special area you can view each time you return. There's never a dull moment at HealthSCOUT—the site skips hospital talk in favor of catchy headlines like "Putting your fat in the fire" and "Grow your own liver."

The Nicholas Institute of Sports Medicine and Athletic Trauma
www.nismat.org

NISMAT
Nicholas Institute of Sports Medicine and Athletic Trauma

This is a no-frills sports medicine site that caters, as one might expect, to the more serious-minded athlete rather than the casual jogger. The site offers lots of advice for dealing with common sports injuries with step-by-step instructions and pictures. Amateurs eyeing the big time will like the site's training tips that focus on enhancing performance and preventing pain. If you don't find what you're looking for there are links to other specialized sports medicine sites to boot.

SxSportsMed.com www.sxsportsmed.com

SxSportsMed.com's articles on fitness and injury prevention speak to a range of athletes from novices to Olympians—there are even a few articles of interest to non-athletes, like a story on high school gym class (who can't relate to that?). The information is broken down by body part, sport, and injury, making it easy to get articles, stretches, and a product solution catalogue tailored to specific problems. If your issue isn't addressed, email a question to the trainers and get a response in 24 hours.

Delicious Decisions www.deliciousdecisions.org

You might think a site linking the adjectives "delicious" and "nutritious" would suck the fun out of eating, but Delicious Decisions manages to come up with a few surprises. Fueled by the American Heart Association, the site focuses on healthy options, not restrictions, so the standard guidelines are accompanied by amazing low fat recipes like bite-sized pizza and pesto spread. There are also some helpful tips on becoming a discerning shopper and tackling the dilemma of dining out.

Outdoorhealth.com www.outdoorhealth.com

Addressing outdoor health in its broadest sense, this site covers the prevention and treatment of backpackers', campers', and explorers' common maladies. Most of the information here is truly useful, like how to help insect stings or remove a tick, though it occasionally strays to topics like childbirth in the wild. To stay on course, head to the Activity-Related Concerns section and scroll down—you'll find that persevering through the technical writing and gruesome pics will get you the first-aid know-how you need.

Centers for Disease Control and Prevention www.cdc.gov

A trustworthy source for sports injury information that parents in particular will love, the Centers for Disease Control's site offers a rundown of sports-specific injuries beneath its A-Z health topics listing. The tips on prevention are basically common sense, but they're backed by an amazing compilation of statistics and references to more sources. Kids are specifically addressed in almost every entry, in addition to a separate "sports injuries among kids" section.

Healthology www.healthology.com

Even-handed daily coverage of trendy health issues as well as more traditional ones is what Healthology offers. Read an article on yoga, tune in to a RealAudio discussion on cancer, or see a live webcast of penile implant surgery. The feel is consumer-oriented, with an energetic tone and a noticeable absence of confusing jargon. And you don't even have to make an appointment to get an answer—the site's experts respond to emails before, during, and after scheduled programs.

Nutrio.com www.nutrio.com

Nutrio.com may not have endorsements from British royals, but it does have enough content to get you on your way to weight loss quickly and safely. You'll drop by for the educational features, but you'll stay for the online tools, which help you formulate a fitness and nutrition program based on your lifestyle. Registration is free and required for some features, but there's still plenty for those who prefer to lurk—like shopping Nutrio.com's partners for helpful products at discounted rates.

PersonalMD.com www.personalmd.com

Pain is part of every athlete's life, but getting an injury treated can often be even worse. At times like these, it's good to have PersonalMD.com, a one-stop shop for medical information and diagnosis. Find everything from profiles of everyday treatments like Ben-Gay to an interactive segment with sports medicine specialists. Learn how to perform without pain with a number of health and fitness features—it doesn't replace a real trainer, but it certainly comes close.

hockey

NHL.com www.nhl.com ©

If your idea of 'slashing' has absolutely nothing to do with hockey sticks, you might want to skip the National Hockey League's official Web site—or pay a visit to their Hockey U link for some continuing education. But for those who know and love the sport that made Gretzky famous (or is it the other way around?), the site is a must-see, offering schedules, breaking news, interviews with coaches and players, video highlights of crucial games ... even a section devoted entirely to kids.

Hockey Hall of Fame www.hhof.com

Imagine ripping the roof off the Hockey Hall of Fame and peering down inside. That's the view afforded by the museum's awesome Web site. Virtual visitors can click around the floor plan to see exhibits, info on inducted players, a hefty audio and video vault, even art that celebrates the sport. Don't miss the 360-degree panoramic views of the trophy room.

CCM www.ccmsports.com ⓓ

If you're serious enough to invest in CCM gear, you'll probably want to try it on before buying. As such, the fact that the company's site is simply a Flash-intensive showroom of slick pictures and specs—without online shopping—doesn't detract. Window shop for skates, pads, and apparel here, and then use the dealer finder to take the next step. Questions on sizing and maintenance are answered in the FAQ.

USA Hockey www.usahockey.com

Casual fans may not find much to entice them at the home of the official governing body for American hockey, but players and coaches will feel right at home. National men's and women's teams of all ages are covered, and there are lots of tips, regulations, and rules to read, right down to the correct specifications for a regulation playing surface. There's even a section on inline hockey for those who prefer the asphalt to the ice.

hockeyinjuries.com www.hockeyinjuries.com

If you play the sport, you might as well make this your homepage. Tackling that inevitable side effect of hockey—pain—hockeyinjuries.com offers tips for addressing smaller injuries yourself and a (somewhat sparse) listing of sports clinics around the country for larger ones. The coolest feature may be the injury calculator, which uses age, injury, and severity to estimate when you can return to the ice. The site also analyzes NHL Injury Reports—find out if you and your favorite players have broken the same bones!

U.S. College Hockey Online www.uscollegehockey.com

You probably know about basketball's Final Four, but do you know the Frozen Four? You will after visiting U.S. College Hockey Online, home to NCAA Division I, II, and III competition for men and women. The design doesn't dazzle but the depth of content is impressive, with stats and news alongside in-depth features and player spotlights. The site will even help you track players' ascension into the bright lights of the NHL with draft coverage and alumni reports.

MyHockeyWorld.com www.myhockeyworld.com

Following hockey is a fun pastime, but how about taking home $15,000 just for tracking events on the ice? It can happen at MyHockeyWorld.com, a site dedicated to fantasy and pool play. Users set up their own leagues or betting systems, or pay a fee and have the work done for them—up to and including game-by-game stat tracking. When tracking your "investments," take advantage of the email newsletter or check out one of many charts and graphs.

Hockey's Future www.hockeysfuture.com

The name may be Hockey's Future, but you'll learn more about the present state of the sport here than you ever imagined possible. Loads of daily updates on both domestic and international hockey keep you abreast of comings and goings among players and coaches. Activity is particularly fierce around draft time, and you'll find all sorts of guides and scouting reports to help you complete your fantasy team or simply stay informed. It's not pretty to look at, but like a grizzled veteran, it gets the job done.

Inline Hockey Central www.inlinehockeycentral.com

INLINE HOCKEY CENTRAL
ALONE IN FRONT

You don't have to be an American skater to use this resource—Inline Hockey Central targets an international crowd in its coverage of leagues and teams. It's especially valuable for those looking to get off the sidelines and is loaded with schedules for tournaments, clinics, and camps. Drawbacks? The much-hyped feature articles sometimes fall short and the news isn't always, well, new.

International Hockey League www.theihl.com

Baseball has the minor leagues, basketball has the CBA, and the NHL has the IHL. The site for the International Hockey League—with teams in locales like Detroit, Manitoba, and Orlando—starts things off with a bang, thanks to a cool intro. After that, it's all the standard stats, team and player profiles, and league information. You'll learn plenty about the up-and-coming stars of hockey, and even find juicy sound bites from the playoffs, when the action is always hottest.

U.S. Field Hockey Association www.usfieldhockey.com

The U.S. Field Hockey site's biggest strength may be its ability to send viewers elsewhere. The homepage offers links to national and club teams, international games (like the Olympics), and a mass of offline tours, tournaments, clinics, and summer camps. Feature content is sparse, though you will find news, field hockey history, and an About Hockey section that covers rules, equipment, and umpiring. The idea seems to be to get both fans and players away from their keyboards and onto the field.

National Hockey League Player's Association www.nhlpa.com

Lending a voice to the people behind the pucks, the NHL player's page counts interviews, biographies, and a player's playbook among its more serious fare. However, the overall focus is towards the young at heart—you'll find Shockwave games and baby pictures of the players here as well. In fact, the Kids section may be the best part of all. The top shelf of its video library has technique tutorials, while the bottom shelf contains clips from *The Hockey Show*.

NewYorkRangers.com www.newyorkrangers.com

Gretzky. Messier. Sather. All the big names connected with the New York Rangers in recent years decorate the team's official homepage. Surfing here will get you their stats, high-tech profiles, and an unexpectedly lush variety of feature articles and multimedia. A huge library of photos, audio, and video clips is browsable by individual player or coach, or type of play (defense or offense)—our search on Mark Messier turned up 13 different documents. Have RealPlayer or QuickTime on hand when you visit.

In The Crease www.inthecrease.com ©

Eight columnists and a hardy affection for hockey make In The Crease a must-read, with regular features like Future Watch and A Look Back that tackle hockey's past and future. The news section offers 10 headlines per day for each of eight leagues. It might not be a pretty site, but the amount of content certainly makes up for it.

Leafnet www.torontomapleleafs.com
It's your best inside look at the Toronto team short of being drafted. In the multimedia area, users can follow games in progress with the live GameCast, an e-tool that combines statistics tickers, play-by-play descriptions and shot charts of the action. Links to live sports radio and a library of 70 video clips highlighting last season's crowd-rousing plays are also located there. Only the Leafwear store is lacking–it contains only a catalogue request form instead of merchandise.

New Jersey Devils www.newjerseydevils.com
Though outsiders might find it corny, true Devils devotees will love reliving their team's 2000 Stanley Cup win when they visit this site with video clips, pictorial celebrations, and audio interviews of the players. The site serves up a healthy dose of non-Stanley Cup features as well, like inside news and behind-the-scenes footage. Die-hards can get ahead on the season with a sneak peek at next year's schedule.

The Dallas Stars www.dallasstars.com
A while has passed since the Dallas Stars last won the Stanley Cup, but they still have their eyes on the prize, and visitors to the team's Web page will, too. The site features a virtual Stanley cup for fans to salivate over–you can manipulate every dimension of hockey's holy grail. But if that's not enough for you, there are also season records, info on trades, and team facts. The design is rather confrontational, but then again, so is the sport.

indoor sports

CollegeBowling.com www.collegebowling.com
Some college bowling teams have been known to pay more attention to their Bud Light than their ball, but not the ones listed here. This site hosts a virtual community for enthusiastic college bowlers and their coaches, with forums full of recent postings, technique advice, and information on upcoming events. Some parts of the site are still undergoing renovation (hence the minimalist design), so check the older version while the new one fills out.

SquashTalk.com www.squashtalk.com
"So you've heard about squash and you want to try it out…" So starts the beginner's guide at SquashTalk, a step-by-step resource that equips newbies with the rules, necessary gear, and tips from the pros. Not everything here is so basic, however–equipment reviews, extensive tourney listings, and drills (in the Improve Yourself section) would help even advanced players better their games. The only thing the site suffers for is a better design and some multimedia (the videos section is full of VHS tapes for sale, not free QuickTime movies).

Bowl.com www.bowl.com

Get your bobby socks and pomade ready. Bowl.com, the recreational bowling world's mega-site, leaves no stone unturned. Though most of its content is devoted to tournament information, there are practical features as well. Find a coach in your area, or chat away on Bowling Talk, where you'll find a vast array of discussion topics from women's bowling to marketing for proprietors.

playpool.com www.playpool.com

It won't make your shot any better, but it's got the rest of the game covered. playpool.com can link you up to a place to play, a person to teach you, and a tournament to test your mettle. The massive pool hall finder turned up 136 different venues within 25 miles of the zip code we tried. playpool.com also features a slew of useful, practical tools pool players can download—check out the variety of tournament planners and score sheets, all available for free.

Bull's Eye News Magazine www.bullsinet.com

You don't have to work the tournament circuit to find out the latest on the darting scene; *Bull's Eye* magazine—to darters as *Wired* is to geeks—fills its site with a satisfying chunk of its print content. The latest news on the game and its players, event results, and columns from field correspondents are among the content. Web-savvy readers will also find online-only features like a nationwide tournament calendar and a growing archive of past articles (with recent issues archived more consistently than earlier ones).

The Billiard Channel.com www.thebilliardchannel.com

Cue sports may not lead ESPN broadcasts or make *Sports Illustrated* covers, but this enthusiastic site easily tops many of the Web pages of more popular sports. The articles here are offbeat and up-tempo—enjoyable reads even if you've never seen a billiards table. After perusing the news, reviews, and highlights sections, viewers should make it a point to download the RealPlayer interviews with players. Sections of the page are still growing as its TV counterpart expands, so you may encounter empty pages.

United States Fencing Association www.usfencing.org

No fencing question is too basic at this site, which answers everything from "What is it?", to "Where can I buy equipment?" and "Where do I fence?" The official Web page for the USFA—the people who train Olympic competitors—is mostly a bulletin board for the organization, but also a good jumping off point for netizens interested in taking up fencing. It holds directions for training camps and competitions, a list of national rankings, and a huge library of links to more online resources.

USA Badminton www.usabadminton.org

Badminton is the world's fastest racket sport; a shuttle can leave the racket at almost 200 mph. If you're not quite up to speed, the official site for USA Badminton can find you a coach or a club and a list of local courts where you can practice. There's not much here in the way of tips or lessons, but plenty of information on the national and international teams and their tournaments.

WorldSport Table Tennis www.tabletennis.worldsport.com ©

If you think table tennis just doesn't get its share of media coverage, look here. Table tennis gets the full treatment in this well-designed instructional site, with timely features, tournament coverage, fitness tips, and news from around the world. Beginners who don't know an anti-loop from a chop should check out the site's glossary of table tennis terms, game regulations, and a history that assumes you're starting from ground zero.

international sports

Sports.com www.sports.com ©

With sports coverage for internationally-minded folk, Sports.com keeps track of it all: football, cricket, golf, tennis, rugby, Formula 1 car racing, and cycling, with tips for bettors. The news is oriented toward European sports, providing links to popular pastimes in Germany, France, Spain, and Italy (clicking on the U.S. links patches you through to CBS SportsLine). Live scores and updates allow you to quickly find the stats you need, and topic-specific bulletin boards let you sound off about that *fútbol* game.

SportingLife www.sporting-life.com

You'll think the British sports pages just exploded across your screen. Unlike what you'll see in the newspaper however, SportingLife.com pairs an easily navigable format with access to over three years of reports and stats, along with a detailed betting section. The site has an amazing breadth of coverage, with hard-hitting articles on cricket, rugby, and a host of other sports.

WorldSport www.worldsport.com © ⓓ ⓞ

There are sports on this site that you've probably never heard of: bandy, korfball, pelota vasca, sambo, and wushu are just some of the selections you can choose from on its lengthy table of contents. No fear, though; sports like football, baseball, and hockey are included, too. The content is simply breathtaking, and the sleek, simple design makes WorldSport a pleasure to search.

Cricket Unlimited www.cricketunlimited.co.uk ©

Sick of watching baseball players dribbling tobacco juice and scratching themselves? Then check out Cricket Unlimited, where the competition is just as fierce but not nearly as vulgar. All kidding aside, this is a great resource for cricket fans who want breaking news, live scores, and players' stats. There's also extensive coverage of the World Cup, as well as articles and interviews with the players.

SportLive www.sportlive.net
The ticker at the top offers a quantifiable measure of this portal's content—when we visited, there were more than 145,000 articles in the site's archive. The emphasis is on sports of interest to Brits, with snooker, Scottish football, and cricket tossed in among mainstays like rugby, tennis, and golf. Users who register can create an online diary, which is simply a personalized page of the news that interests them, or a Web page for their own amateur team in the Grassroots section.

Sportal www.sportal.com
Sportal, a solid network of international sports sites, does just what its name implies: it allows you to hop from portal to portal to check out sports coverage in different countries. Well-written and updated articles address all of the major sports in Germany, Sweden, France, and Spain (among others), and exclusive audio interviews let you hear the players' takes on the latest games. If you'd like to get Sportal's goods on your WAP device, the thorough mobile section will take you through the steps.

petanque.org www.petanque.org
Petanque, lawn bowling's French cousin, may be obscure enough to draw blank stares at the local sports bar, but players in 30 countries seriously play it. petanque.org contains a fairly solid mix of information pertaining to the game—rules, news, profiles of global matches, and descriptions of various shots—and while some sections want for lack of attention, most are regularly updated. There is even a stilted translation of the original French rules: "a shooter who is about to shoot a *boule* must before shooting shout 'watch out' to warn the public."

Scrum.com www.scrum.com
Scrum (n): the formation used in the setplay restarting play after a knock-on or forward pass. Did you get all that? If you did, you're one of the devout fans that will value this wing of the Sportal network, where attention is lavished on rugby players (including students and women), games, and tournaments. The 40 Q & A's found in the site's archives are characteristic of the amount of content on the site as a whole.

Planet Rugby www.planet-rugby.com
Planet Rugby seems to follow the theory that you can never get too much of a good thing; the site bombards users with loads of news, results, match commentary, and a database of tournament information that goes back to 1871. We appreciate the thoroughness, but we also recommend using the site's News and Players search engines to find what you want within the mass. There is also a News by Country option, for a manageable page on a specific nation's rugby scene.

Eurosport www.eurosport.com
A portal for international sports that takes full advantage of Net technology. Each of Eurosport's 12 sports receives its own subpage and a crop of interactives like live coverage, video highlights, and more text than would be manageable offline. Even the daily news in the News Room comes in RealPlayer segments (with an archive that has months of past clips). Head to the Forum section for more than just a chat venue—it's where the free newsletter, shopping, and games are located.

CricketLine.com www.cricketline.com

The most interesting element in cricket—the players—gets the most extensive treatment on this site, with an amazing database that addresses every person to swing professionally. Cool, interactive tools, or "facilities" as they're known to the British, make it easy to compare stats and see how different players stack up. The site also frequently posts news updates, with special sections for games in Bangladesh, Pakistan, Sri Lanka, and six other countries as well as England.

African Sports www.africansports.com
While many sites define "global" as Europe and the U.S., African Sports actually offers coverage outside those two continents. Viewers can choose any of 21 specific sports listed, or use the SportsScheduler to easily track the continent's major teams and African club and national competitions. It's mostly straight up news, and mostly soccer news at that, but the site is extremely up to date and comes direct from each of 30 countries' local news sources.

martial arts

Body Mind & Modem www.bodymindandmodem.com ⓓ ⓞ
This site aims to jumpstart your inner peace by demonstrating relaxation techniques based on the Japanese martial art Aikido. Still photos and (sometimes grainy) videos show you what each exercise looks like, while the accompanying text outlines tips for good form. But lest you think the site takes itself too seriously, there are also fun (if improbable) features on such topics as cool cocktail party tricks.

Martialinfo.com www.martialinfo.com

Newcomers: head straight to read the Newbie Guide to Martial Arts Training or check out New Here for a Martial Arts FAQ. Once you've mastered the basics, read features like "Chinese martial arts" and "Kung fu fighting in America." Check out the Who's Who and the Hall of Fame for the latest names, the Styles section to find out which martial arts style is best for you. Though some may find the format ghastly, the wealth of info and links make it a worthwhile stop for newbies and masters alike.

AikiWeb www.aikiweb.com

Make the mind-body-spirit connection with a couple of strategic clicks. AikiWeb balances the psychology of the Japanese martial art Aikido with technique, so you'll find great articles on spirituality as well as tips for optimum training. Newcomers will like the Japanese language instruction section with audio clips to aid pronunciation, while pros will appreciate tips on keeping gear stain free. Humor is present, as well—one can't take the tips on "bowling the Aikido" way too seriously.

Black Belt www.blackbeltmag.com

The editors of *Black Belt Magazine*, the offline bible of martial arts, have established an impressive presence on the Internet as well. Highlights include "What combat system is right for you?" and the all-important "How to choose the right martial arts school." A great section for kids and a handy glossary of martial arts terms rounds out the site. A special members-only area is also available for $4.95 a month.

Internation TaeKwon-Do Association www.itatkd.com

According to its practitioners, tae kwon do brings fluidity to motion and a path to physical harmony. If you'd like to try it, this site's Animated Techniques section demonstrates some of the moves, while the more philosophical side of tae kwon do (tenets, oath, etiquette) is addressed under the Information heading. The site also serves as a clearinghouse for the International TaeKwon-Do Association, providing information about the ITA to instructors and students, and a means for members to communicate with ITA Headquarters.

Bushido Online www.bushido.ch

Bushido—literally translated as "the way of the warrior"—is considered by some to be the starting point for all martial arts. The site provides information on all Bushido-related news, facts, and a list of current events. The site also serves as a clearinghouse for other disciplines, with the history of karate, kung fu, and kobudo.

Martial-arts.com www.martial-arts.com

Never thought you could kick your way to a black belt online? Think again. At Martial-arts.com aspiring masters can sign up for virtual martial arts classes (from kick boxing to karate) and get fit with weekly health features on basics like sleep, asthma, and muscle soreness. While you're cooling down post-session, read up on your favorite martial arts veterans, or peruse the site's small shopping section for essentials like headgear and groin guards.

NASCAR Online www.nascar.com ©

Just how did Jeffery Bodine survive that last crash? The official site of the National Association of Stock Car Racing puts you in the center of the action with interviews, driver profiles, and news straight from the pit. NASCAR Online also has qualifying results and schedules, as well as an interactive Garage section with Shockwave games that illustrate the different parts of a race car and technical stuff like the effects of tire pressure on handling. Note: the news section has breaking stories; the newsstand just wants to sell you magazine subscriptions.

SpeedFX.com www.speedfx.com

Managing five separate racing challenges (Winston Cup, Busch Series, Truck Series, ASA, and ARCA) might seem tricky, but this arm of the RacingOne.com network is up to the task. Surf here for recent and past race results, points standings, team profiles, and a full schedule of upcoming events on each. Be sure to peruse the terrific collection of editorials by this site's columnists, posting on topics like car sponsorship and the most impressive rookies this season. The Viewpoint link has an archive of previous columns.

That's Racin' www.thatsracin.com ©

Want to find out how close Terry Labonte came to winning the 1997 Pepsi 400? No problem. That's Racin' contains a database of all the major NASCAR races dating back to 1996, including commentary on each race and a round-up of the top finishers. Also in the database is a listing of major raceways in America, complete with directions to get there and area attractions.

Formula I Online www.f1.on.net

For fans of grit and speed, Formula 1 Online is beyond comprehensive in its racing coverage. Choose from an array of live races to watch, read about great drivers past and present, or gab with other racing nuts. You'll even find wallpaper for your PC background in the Downloads section.

Speedvision Network www.speedvision.com

Motorcycle racing is often given short shrift on racing sites, but Speedvision Network provides extensive coverage of AMA Motorcross, Supercross, and Superbike, F-USA Dirt Track and more, along with all the latest industry news, schedules and race results. Motor boat racing coverage includes scores and a parts and accessories store. Add full coverage of Aviation, F1, CART, NASCAR, NHRA and IRL to the mix and this site has speed covered.

CART.com www.cart.com ©

CART is the open-wheel champ in the U.S. and this site (part of the Quokka Sports network) manages to convey just about everything except the smell of burning fuel. This official site has access to all the CART drivers, so expect plenty of exclusive video and print interviews with all the top drivers. Coverage includes both qualifying events and major race news, plus team and driver stats. Die-hard fans should check the site out on race day, when it serves up real-time racing updates.

ATLAS F1 www.atlasf1.com

Are these folks F1 fanatics? After seeing the countdown clock, we'd have to say so. It tells exactly how many minutes until the next Grand Prix. Fans looking to pass the time until the next race should hang out at this site, packed with all sorts of stats, drivers' biographies, test time summaries, and funny tips like a guide to differentiating between drivers on the same team. The archives are packed full of past titles, as are the forums (one heading lists just under 60,000 postings!).

RacingOne.com www.racingone.com

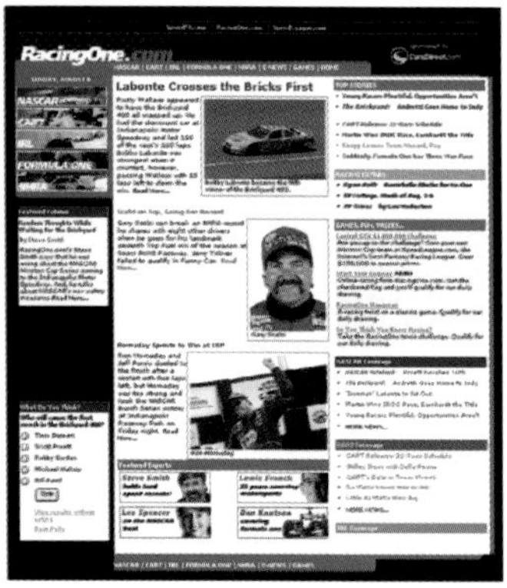

While many sites feature the latest results, few can match RacingOne.com's concentration on feature articles. Titles like "Indy is F1's best chance at U.S. success" and "The king of speed returns to Daytona" offer an insider perspective on NASCAR, CART, IRL, F1 and NHRA drivers and industry gossip. If you'd like to hear about the latest news as it happens, subscribe to RacingOne.com's E-News, sit back, and wait for the "big breaking news" to come to you.

ESPN.com Auto Racing www.espn.go.com/auto

If you're always missing the results of your favorite races, visit ESPN.com and produce your own personal highlight reel using the ESPN.com video clips (you'll find at least a handful of clips available for your viewing pleasure). Or stop at the NASCAR store, offering 1:24 scale die-cast cars, T-shirts and hats for fans of virtually any driver. ESPN.com knows all motor sports, of course, so also look for standings and results for other favorites like Formula 1, CART, and NASCAR.

The Jalopy Journal www.jalopyjournal.com

This throwback to the days of pin-up girls and chrome bumpers offers a community-oriented look into the world of rodding. The Bench Rodding section lets members wax nostalgic about past cars and races, while the Feature Cars shows slide shows of this month's hot wheels. See the classifieds if you're in the market to buy a car and join the community.

PlanetF1.com www.planet-f1.com
Hakkinen may have beaten Schumacher in the last race, but what about the five before that? See how the career stats of any two drivers compare by plugging their names into the Head to Head tool here. The list of names extends back to1950, though it only works for racers who have actually driven against each other. Other surf-worthy material includes a Technical Focus column, next year's driver lineup, and two e-newsletters: Planet F1 Weekly for those who want a weekly breakdown, and Planet Race Update for those who want to be buried up to their eyeballs in race-day Grand Prix developments.

Indy Racing Online www.indyracing.com
Indy 500 may be the race most have heard of, but Tony George's Indy Racing League encompasses an entire series of open-wheel races. The official IRL site is the place to check for the latest race results, driver standings, photo galleries, and team reports for races in Phoenix, Texas, and Las Vegas, among others. If you get lost amongst the ads on the homepage—similar in number to those on the race cars themselves—use the links to click directly to specific races.

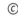

outdoors & camping

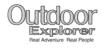

Outdoor Explorer www.outdoorexplorer.com ©
The smell of pine trees, the clean mountain air, the sound of rushing water… Who needs it when you have Outdoor Explorer? The site has so much hiking, climbing, mountain biking, river sports, and skiing-related content that you might never make it outside. You'll find well-wrought, informative articles, travel advice, gear shopping and swapping, and a regional weekend calendar, all packed into a low-key design that doesn't distract.

Outside Online www.outsidemag.com ©
Skateboard queen Cara-Beth Burnside and the members of the NYPD scuba unit don't appear to have a lot in common, except for the shared enthusiasm for outdoor activities that got them featured here. *Outside Magazine*'s Web site is more than just a glorified archive of articles from the magazine, though you'll find plenty of past features distributed throughout. Each of the Web's different sections is hosted by a personality—Mr. Fit and Gear Guy are two—who dispenses expertise and answers reader questions.

MountainWeb.com www.mountainweb.com
From the famous Flatirons of Boulder, Colorado to New York's Brick Yard trail, MountainWeb.com is the premier site for route and trail descriptions for hiking, backpacking, and mountaineering. We'll forgive it the occasional broken link since the info is so useful—one article on Mt. Saint Helens gave a printable climbing permit application and reservation date information along with the route details. You can also sell your used gear online here or hook up with climbing partners.

ParkNet www.nps.gov ©

Aside from the massive listing of national and local parks in the United States, the National Park Service Web site is a rich educational resource for environmental and geological studies. Articles, photos, and fact sheets, as well as tour guides and contact information, supplement visits to the parks, while a fascinating historical section highlights the importance of conservation and open space. A great tool for teachers.

Backpacker.com www.backpacker.com
Why would one expert hiker sooner pack a carabiner (climber's clip) than a pocket knife? Backpacker.com has the answer in its hefty gear section, as well as repair how-tos, a GearFinder, and reviews of products (like hiking boots) by people who have twisted their ankles enough to know. The site's staff also covers major hiking destinations and ways to stay safe in the wilderness.

GreatOutdoors.com www.greatoutdoors.com ©
A package as tidy as a shiny, new mess kit, GreatOutdoors.com provides a feature article, tips, news, and a BBS forum for each of the outdoor sports it covers. Climbers can read about one man's trip up the Blue Mountains, learn the value of a stick clip, and gather pointers on leading a climb, all in one place. The site can also help you plan your next trip, with destination profiles and advice on the best seasons to visit. Though the articles don't change over nearly as often as you'd hope, the sheer volume of information here just about makes up for it.

Field & Stream and Outdoor Life www.fieldandstream.com ©
This full-service Web version of *Field and Stream* magazine has information to help you brush up on your turkey tactics, decide what deer gear

you'll need this season, and get the latest news on every weapon from primitive bows to cutting-edge optics. Especially helpful are the fish and game finders—choose from the list of animals and the site returns an encyclopedia-like entry on the animal's most notable characteristics and how-to info on the best hunting strategies.

Explore.com www.explore.com © ⓓ ⓞ

A cool primer on the adventure sports scene that covers rough-and-tumble activities like hiking, kayaking, and snowboarding. Explore.com even champions eco-tourism and conservation with articles about earth-smart sports and places in their Enviro section. There are also guides to sporting gear, adventurous travel spots, and various athletic competitions taking place around the world.

GORP.com www.gorp.com ©

The nature site affectionately termed GORP is the information hub for outdoor enthusiasts and action-oriented travelers. Browse featured locations like Yellowstone or Aspen for ideas and inspiration, or scroll down to read useful and practical columns on health, safety, how-to and what-to-see. Shop for gear, book a trip, find a trail; GORP does everything but tie your hiking boots for you.

Active.com www.active.com © ⓞ

Arranged by region, Active USA has information on sporting events and competitions taking place around the country. Practically every sport conceivable is listed, from fencing to snowshoeing to waterskiing. Events for disabled athletes are listed as well. If nothing exciting is going on in your area, you can always check out the feature stories, which you can search by sport.

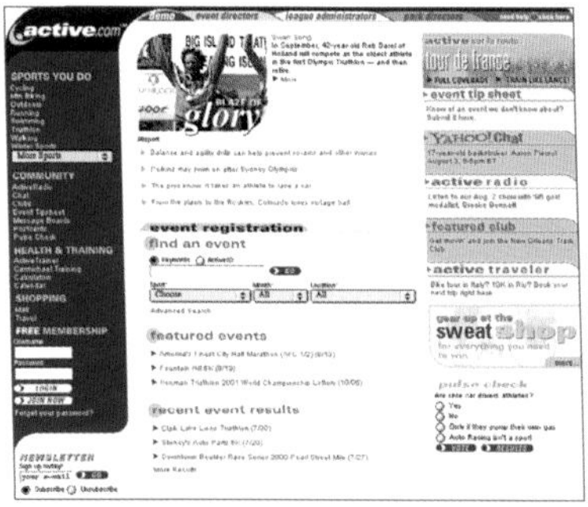

thebackpacker.com www.thebackpacker.com

You may not be ready to retrace the journey of Lewis and Clark, but if you're at all inclined to hike, there's something for you here. thebackpacker.com covers every aspect of hiking, with a special section for beginners that explains water filters, trail etiquette, Gore-Tex, and other essentials. The site's trail database is also exemplary—listings include state and region (i.e. northeast Washington), length and difficulty of the trail, and driving directions. But perhaps you'd rather walk?

Campmor www.campmor.com © ⓓ

Keep your toes toasty and save the Appalachian Trail at the same time. Among Campmor's superior selection of insulated sleeping bags, hiking boots, compasses, and kitchenware, the site also lists a $2 donation toward saving the threatened trail that shoppers can pop in their shopping carts. Considering Campmor's sizeable Web specials—one $160 North Face jacket was marked down to $80 when we visited—you'll doubtless be able to afford the contribution.

Eastern Mountain Sports www.shopems.com © ⓢ

Save your energy for the hike—get your supplies at Eastern Mountain Sports. The site has an enormous variety of equipment, apparel, and info for every outdoor adventure from bird watching to mountain biking. Activity-specific supply checklists provide foolproof preparedness for whatever outing you may be attempting; the site also provides detailed sizing information for clothes, hats, shoes, sleeping bags, and backpacks in the Fitting Area.

beOutdoors.com www.beoutdoors.com

You're sitting at the desk in your cubicle, alphabetizing the company's take-out menus and organizing your paper clips by size. It's time to visit beOutdoors.com and plan a weekend getaway. It's got everything you need to go boating, fishing, hunting, or camping, plus refresher courses on the dos and don'ts of outdoor sports. The customer service information here is almost too thorough; look up how to return a product and beOutdoors.com returns a 13-point checklist of information you must provide. Don't know about you, but we'd rather be fishing!

The Virtual Flyshop www.flyshop.com

Wind your hackle backward to make a better dry fly—so advises The Virtual Flyshop, a fishing e-zine that delves into the nuances of fly fishing like fly tying, rod building, and identifying different mayfly hatches. Feature articles accompany steady columns on each of the aforementioned skills, and all are updated every few days. You'll also find books, videos, and software in the Media Source, though the e-commerce section actually links through to 13 different tackle equipment sites.

US Orienteering Federation www.us.orienteering.org

Orienteering makes being lost an art form. Practitioners of the sport use detailed maps and a compass to find their way through the woods on foot, bike, or ski. The U.S. Orienteering Federation site offers a full listing of local chapters, as well as details on the latest events in state parks, national forests, and local recreation areas. Visit the Education section to learn how to really use your compass, or to brush up on orienteering lingo with the visual glossary.

Away.com www.away.com

Away.com is a site for those of us who need to get away from it all but don't know where to go. Designed with outdoorsy adventure-seekers in mind, it recommends outings like horseback riding, mountaineering, and ecotourism. Choose a place and the site presents activities; choose an activity and it lists the best places to do it. Want to party? Look to the 1,001 festivals section for world-wide options. Drawing a complete blank? Check the idea generator.

The U.S. Fish and Wildlife Service www.fws.gov

An annual count of around 35 million fishermen and 14 million hunters would add up to an unbalanced ecosystem if it wasn't for the U.S. Fish and Wildlife Service. The agency's Web site is a detailed and fact-filled repository of information that can point sportsmen to hunting and fishing destinations, and steer them around reserves. It also has the official word on laws and regulations, and can direct hunters in need of a permit to their state's Web page.

Trails.com www.trails.com
The quickest way to find hiking and mountain biking destinations in your area, Trails.com sports a Trail Finder database with 10,000 unique listings, sortable by location, difficulty, length, and duration. When you find a trail that looks promising, print out a Topo Map of the path's topography, and use the Trip Planner to organize a group to go with you. Trails.com also offers an extensive e-commerce wing with 4,000 kinds of books, maps, and gear.

TrailSource www.trailsource.com
TrailSource is like four Web sites in one, with detailed trail information for mountain biking, cross-country skiing, hiking, and snowboarding. Each of the hundreds of entries includes directions to the individual trails, the best seasons to use them, local lodging (if any), and links to any guidebooks that might be available. Use the Meccas link to view the staff's seasonal picks for essential outdoor destinations, but steer clear of the sponsors disguised as services on the homepage's left side.

All Outdoors www.alloutdoors.com
Looking for a site as big as all outdoors? Here it is. Though this portal's emphasis is on hunting and fishing, it seems they've put in a little of everything outdoors. Expect to find advice on adventure travel, what to feed your bird dog, and recipes (like Snapper Vegetable Soup, as in snapping turtle) mixed in with more conventional content. The Coffee Shop has forums for connecting with other grizzled hunters, fishers, and firearms enthusiasts, and the Trading Post and newsstand both offer shopping.

National Recreation Reservation Service
www.reserveusa.com
Now this is true innovation—reserving a camping space online! If you're an outdoorsy type who likes to plan ahead, The National Recreation Reservation Service provides directions, site amenities, availability, and rates for thousands of campgrounds across the U.S. For the less hardy, there are half a dozen states that offer federal cabins for rent.

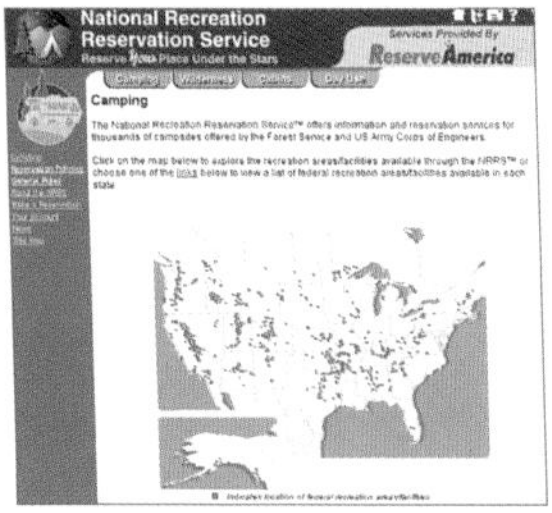

WomenOutdoors.com www.womenoutdoors.com
Specially designed for women with an active streak, WomenOutdoors.com will help you get suited up for your next adventure. A handy drop-down menu helps you shop by sport, department, or brand name for everything from parkas to hibernation sleeping bags. Gear guides abound, but specific questions can also be answered by Nancy, the site's in-house expert. Aside from gear, find interesting features on things like trail running in the nation's capital, kayaking honeymoons, and for the particularly brave, how to take your kids with you.

Altrec.com www.altrec.com © ⓓ ⓢ

For the outdoor enthusiast who never goes inside, Altrec.com invites surfers to experience the great outdoors, plan for trips, and chat with fellow adventurers before choosing their gear. The articles and travel advisories here are intelligent and far better than most sports sites we've seen. Altrec.com will even help you accessorize and color-coordinate an ensemble with clothes, packs, and assorted gadgets in matching earth tones.

portals

ESPN.com www.espn.go.com © ⓓ

A-list sports news, fantasy games, athlete interviews... ESPN.com is as comprehensive as one might imagine it would be, for mainstream American sports at least. The columns and news coverage here will keep you coming back for more (as will the game schedules), and you can register for their Community to chat with other fans or just play online games.

HighWired.com www.highwiredsports.com

Billing itself as America's online high school network, HighWired.com profiles local and regional high school athletics, giving equal billing to extra-curriculars like gymnastics and golf alongside coverage of football, soccer, basketball, and more. Click on the Inside Sports link to read about up-and-coming players, and the Recruiting link for tips on how to make college teams. The camp and tournament finders are also useful.

Total Sports www.totalsports.net ©

What makes Total Sports so cool? Beyond the standard news and features, Total Sports offers TotalCast coverage of in-progress games. Select the game you want to watch (from NCAA basketball to major league baseball) and the site provides a companion window with game status, statistics, play-by-play coverage, a real-time scoreboard, and photos. There's no video provided, but TotalCasts are perfect as a companion to watching a game on TV, or for tracking a game while at work.

CNNSI.com www.cnnsi.com © ⓓ

Bathing suits, sports, and... more bathing suits. Brought to you by a partnership of CNN and *Sports Illustrated*, CNNSI.com serves up all the features you love in the print publication, plus fancy multimedia tools you'll wonder how you did without. Check the daily news headlines, watch footage of game highlights, listen to interviews with players, or chat with other sports fans. And don't miss the swimsuit gallery, which contains archives, Web-exclusive pictures, and even a zoom button.

The Sporting News Online www.sportingnews.com ©

Rare is the sports fan that needs complete and up-to-date information on all 700 pro and college teams, but if you can take it, The Sporting News Online will dish it out. The site's personalization feature lets users tailor the homepage to include news on some, none, or all of the teams it keeps track of. You can also choose which columnists' weekly rants you want to read, as well as whether you want to receive the updates via email.

Rivals.com www.rivals.com ⓞ

Rivals.com, an online sports network, satisfies even the most rabid athletic appetite with the scoop on more than 500 sports teams and semi-independent sites covering everything from professional hoops to competitive skateboarding. Get the score on national football recruiting or hear the blow-by-blow of the last Flyers hockey match. Expert commentary digs deep, and videos of key plays and game rebroadcasts make Rivals.com an indispensable resource.

FOXSports.com www.foxsports.com ©

The wide world of sports just got wider. FOXSports.com is loaded with coverage of professional, college and high school hockey, hoops, auto racing, football, baseball, soccer, golf, tennis, and more. Streaming video and audio features and lots of hot columnists (like John Madden) set it apart from the run of sports info sites. What can we say? If you need information about sports, you'll find it here.

SportsServer www.sportserver.com

A site that comes close to sports omniscience with an unbelievable amount of stats and schedules for virtually every sport in the United States–right down to arena football and minor league hockey. Even if your interests are more global, there's a link to international coverage of tennis and soccer–pardon, *football*. Check out the Pressbox for columns by the site's sportswriters; there are also chat boards for all you armchair commentators out there.

SportsForWomen.com www.sportsforwomen.com ⓓ

Ladies, let's play. SportsForWomen.com is a community site and info hub that focuses on inspiring women athletes, both professional and amateur. Page through the scrapbook to view their cool collection of user-submitted photos, or click around for news, chat, and updates on all types of women's professional and college sports.

tuneinsports.com www.tuneinsports.com ©

Users who are willing to wait out the five-minute download time get to watch hapless skaters suck asphalt and bikers bite the dust at tuneinsports.com's bloopers section. Naturally, this guide to TV, radio, and online sports coverage has some more serious offerings, including a lengthy list of sports schedules updated daily. Search for your favorite team or browse through all the day's games. The interface can be a little clunky, but the information is timely and useful.

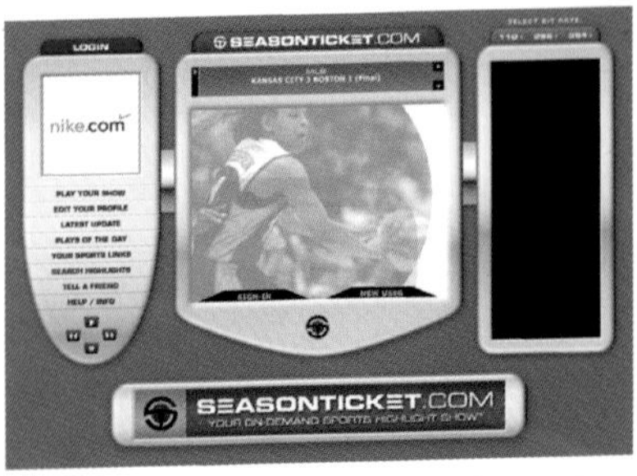

SeasonTicket.com
www.seasonticket.com ⓓ ⓞ

Only the broadband-blessed gain admission to this slick multimedia sports paradise. SeasonTicket.com eliminates the need to sit through the evening news' relentless replaying of Sammy Sosa's home runs. Instead, users create their own customized audio and video highlights shows. Register for free, create a profile in minutes (pick major sports leagues, teams, and time frame), and then sit back and watch plays from the last few days of baseball, football, hockey, soccer, golf, or basketball—it's your choice.

Sportspages.com www.sportspages.com ⓞ

What if you could peruse the sports pages of newspapers all over the world? Rich Johnson's Sportspages.com makes that possible, with sports page links for papers like the *Las Vegas Sun* and the *Hong Kong Standard*, all sorted by region, sport, and league. The Daily Link Service holds Rich's picks for the best sports links on the Web, while weekly trivia features amuse between innings.

SportsJones www.sportsjones.com ⓒ ⓞ

Updated daily, SportsJones will give you a fix on all things athletic. Sections include books, culture and politics, humor, stats and analysis, and interviews. It's definitely quirkier than most sports sites, but that's part of this magazine's appeal. There's lots to explore, but it may be wasted on folks who don't have a sense of humor.

sportsTALK.com www.sportstalk.com ⓒ

Think how dull the world of sports would be without the always-colorful rumors and gossip. The folks at sportsTALK.com have a direct pipeline to all the latest fodder on players, upcoming drafts, rookies to watch, and big names on the slide. Check out the Daily Rumor Mill to find out what their "sources" are saying in the world of the NFL, NBA, NHL, and MLB sports, direct from the horse's mouth, or catch up on player stats and good old regular news.

Quokka Sports www.quokka.com ⓒ ⓞ

Any sport site can give you the scoop from the sidelines, but Quokka Sports wants to get you inside the athlete's head. The site peddles what it calls Quokka Sports Immersion, using video, telemetry, biometrics, GPS data, timing, statistics, and email directly from the competitors to help you experience sports like the athletes do. You'll also find a live coverage section and links to the network's many satellite pages.

AthletesDirect www.athletesdirect.com ⓓ ⓞ

All players, all the time—AthletesDirect serves up a bountiful offering of athlete-specific news and bios. Search by sport or jock and reflect with Rick Fox, bowl with Reggie Jackson, or follow Anna Kournikova around the latest tennis tournament. Use one of the more than 200 links to athlete's official sites to ask your sports hero a question, check his or her stats, or read a first-person story.

Sports News www.sportsnews.com

A lot of "all-in-one" sites claim to cover every sport known to man, but few can touch the selection at Sports News. A handy tool bar offers ready access to climbing, cricket, rugby, snooker, swimming, and volleyball—but that's just the start. The main section also includes baseball, football, hockey, tennis and golf and you'll find all the latest headlines for each. You'll also find handy links to the latest sports news from ABC, BBC, ESPN, and Sporting Life.

International Association of Sports Museums & Halls of Fame
www.sportshalls.com

Where can an up-and-comer go for a little inspiration? How about the International Swimming Hall of Fame, located in Fort Lauderdale, Florida? Sports enthusiasts passing through New York will be pleased to know that there are no less than seven athletic museums in that state. And fans of women's b-ball may just want to plan a trip to Knoxville, Tennessee, where that hall of fame is located. The site isn't merely a bank of addresses; it also has descriptions of the museums it lists.

eSports.com www.esports.com

Pro sports often get all the glory, but the heart of the sporting community is really at the local level. At eSports.com, you'll find plenty of information on neighborhood organizations, little leagues, pick-up games, recreational programs, and house leagues. Registered users can create a Web page for their team, get help organizing a carpool, or download a rules sheet for later use. Start at the site tour to learn how.

CBS SportsLine www.cbs.sportsline.com ©

SportsLine has the corner on comprehensive when it comes to sports sites, providing the same wealth of authoritative information that won your trust in the television channel. But you don't even have to visit the site to get the goods if you grab their free Sports Ticker. The program downloads in less than two minutes and constantly rattles off up-to-the-second details on whichever teams you tell it to track.

Broadcast Sports sports.broadcastamerica.com

An indispensable resource for travelers and displaced fans, Broadcast Sports brings crystal clear live sports radio from all over the globe to your computer. Users can listen to specific regional radio frequencies, programmed streaming radio, or Sports Soundbytes selected by BroadcastAmerica. Download RealPlayer or Windows Media, and then check the Upcoming Events schedule to see what live events are slated for the day.

MouthOffSports.com www.mouthoffsports.com

Truly a monster monster-board, this is a place to post your opinion on everything sports. Topics center around the big pro sports (with smaller sections for trivia and fantasy leagues), and the discussions are extremely active—one post we saw had received 28 responses in just two days. Register first, and then jaw all you want about the Bears' latest loss or your first love (the Red Sox).

Sportcut.com www.sportcut.com

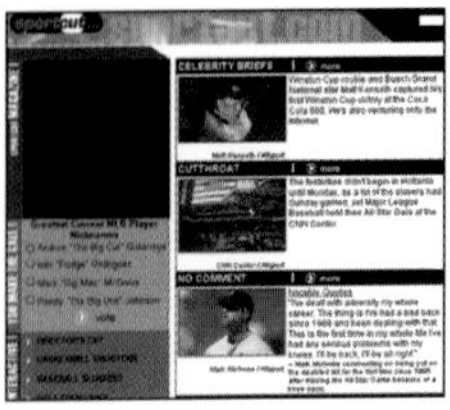

Sports news with an attitude. A real big attitude. Step inside the Sportcut.com Insider for a celebrity-focused slant on sports news—profiles of the hottest, gossip on the worst-behaved, and news on the rest. You can also offer up your own opinion on the aptly named "controversy of the week," or check out (or contribute to) the list of athlete sightings.

Yahoo! Broadcast Sports www.broadcast.com/sports_events

This wing of the popular portal has *TV Guide*-style listings for sports coverage online. Choose a sport to see what's on, or select the medium you prefer—video, radio, television, and broadband each have sections. Press conferences, game coverage, and news footage are some of the things the site links through to. You'll want to have RealPlayer before you begin; the site will walk you through downloading it step by step.

Fidget.com www.fidget.com

Fidget.com is for desk-bound folks who jump for joy every time their email beeps. The site will deliver any of its 1,500 eNewsletters to your inbox on a daily or weekly basis, 30 of which cover sports topics. Sign up to get twice-weekly salvos from Mike Lupica, the infamous columnist from the *New York Daily News*, or weekly opinions from Jeff Savage, the so-called "Howard Stern of sports." Head to the site directory and click on sports for the complete list.

Sports Sleuth www.sportssleuth.com

Sports Sleuth taps sources all over the world to bring surfers the inside scoop on any team or player by email. The site scopes information in hometown papers, team histories, and ESPN so you don't have to. To start the site sleuthing for you, register the teams you would like to track (up to five) and then wait for your daily email message. You'll get the most recent local and national news, game recaps, injury reports, and anything else you'd like to know.

SportsFan Radio www.sportsfanradio.com

Think of it as an Internet radio station and newspaper sports page combined. You'll find a compelling mix of gossip and wrap-ups at SportsFan Radio, where commentaries on baseball, football, basketball, and auto racing are broadcast along with in-depth discussions on the latest trades, bloopers, and big-time players. Programs like *Steve and the Sports Pig*, *The Fabulous Sports Babe*, and *Inside the NHL* are particularly worth a listen.

ZuluSports.com www.zulusports.com © ⓓ

Log on here to behold the myriad ways an athlete can plow through earth, air, water, and snow. It's easy to be seduced by the compact design and flashy headlines of this adventure sports destination—"How Tandem Skydiving is Like Sex With a Stranger," was a recent story. But the content behind the glitz won't disappoint; features are in-depth, gear reviews from users and experts top-notch, and destination coverage wide-ranging (more than 350 different locales are listed).

running

Kick! Sports www.kicksports.com ©

Kick! is a slight misnomer; it's really a site devoted to running, jogging, and racing, none of which involve kicking (if memory serves correctly). However, if you're looking for tips on getting motivated, setting rhythms, or training for a big race, you're sure to find what you need at this site. There are even suggestions for dealing with such annoyances as mad dogs (respect their boundaries, act nuts if attacked) and crazy drivers (same advice).

Runner's World www.runnersworld.com ©

New and innovative ways to wear your Nikes down to rubbery ribbons abound at this online running magazine. The site is aimed at beginning runners and offers counter-arguments to all your worn excuses for staying inside. Register to keep a training log right on the site that the Runner's World staff will look over, critique, and congratulate. Our only complaint is the overzealous effort to get surfers to subscribe to the print magazine—many of the sections are cut short.

Cool Running www.coolrunning.com

Runners that salivate upon hearing the phrase "minimum 40 mile week" will appreciate Cool Running's preference for marathons. What the site does best is connect runners and long-distance races, providing a pull-down menu of printable entry forms for marathons in the next six months. While you won't find many new training tips (some were written in 1997), you can count on the active bulletin board for up-to-the-second advice. When we tried, it took four minutes for our posting to get a response.

Springco Athletics www.springcoathletics.com

A life-saver for the serious track and field enthusiast, Sprinco Athletics specializes in hard-to-find equipment for hard-core running stars. Search by keyword or gear type (training, cross-country, throwing . . .) for your next "steel throwing circles" or nutritional supplements. Easy navigation, plentiful selection, and regular sales make shopping a breeze.

Road Runner Sports www.roadrunnersports.com ©

Road Runner Sports has more than 240,000 shoes available on its site (practically every brand with the notable exception of Nike), plus articles, race registration, an online auction, a runner's club, and products like heart monitors, insoles, water bottles, and nutritional supplements. This site is especially good for new runners seeking the encouragement to go the extra mile; we love the product reviews, injury information, and customized shoe search.

realrunner.com www.realrunner.com ⓓ

A man on a mission, Kim Hongyoung is running around the world (literally) to raise money for Korean athletes. But you don't have to be as extreme in your commitment to distance running to get something out of this site. Its sections range from Starting Out to Ultimate Challenges, with cool tools and articles for everyone in between. The site also lists running clubs and races, as well as contact info for vacation companies that offer trips centered around—you guessed it—running.

Run-Down.com www.run-down.com ©

Run-Down.com gives, what else, a total run-down on the running scene. You'll find little original content, but lots of links that take you to regular updates on college and high school track meets, adult running clubs, Olympic hopefuls, and professional results. Click over to use the Run-Down Training Partner Locator to score a running mate or find local competitions. While not the most glamorous site, it is a good place to begin whether you're pounding real or virtual pavement.

Women's Running www.womens-running.com

In the words of the greatest female cross-country racer in U.S. history, Lynn Jennings, "Mental will is a muscle that needs exercise, just like muscles of the body." Exercise your clicking finger at Women's Running and you'll find more than enough inspiration to make you hit the road again. Run by the people who write the magazine *Runner's World*, this site covers a plethora of women's running issues, from training schedules to how much to run while pregnant.

CollegeRunning.Com www.collegerunning.com © ⓓ

Photo galleries on this fantastic site covering the college running scene provide little-known athletes with more than their fifteen minutes of fame. If you are a prospective student, check the College Programs category for info on the program at your school of choice. Also available are race results, interviews, and a chat room. And if you're a parent, you can check your kid's progress under the Outdoors Results link—just don't expect CollegeRunning.Com to tell you how much the sport is distracting your child from her studies.

skating

K2Skates.com www.k2skates.com ⓓ

A brand name that advanced inline skaters will recognize (and beginners should know), K2's Web site is an animation-based showcase of the popular product line—but you should know up front that you can't actually buy the skates here. Still, anyone who craves a pair of K2s should check it out. The site's Skate Selector steers users to the right pair, the Tech section teaches how to take care of them, and the Tips & Tricks page offers cool ways to impress your friends at the skate park.

Rollerblade www.rollerblade.com © ⓓ

The pioneer of the sport, Rollerblade is still the leader in the in-line skate market. Though the company has yet to offer online shopping, it does provide some substantial content. The Getting Started section runs through safety equipment and hints for beginners, while Skating for Fitness takes on the aerobic aspects of the sport. If you do use the dealer finder and buy a pair, you'll want to check out the maintenance movies here (according to Rollerblade, your skates just want to be loved).

US Figure Skating Online www.usfsa.com ©

Skating information so in-depth, only serious skaters and religious followers of the sport would care to delve into it. The US Figure Skating Association's official Web site is a bit lackluster in terms of graphics, but packs an incomparable amount of newsworthy articles and records into its framework. Skater profiles are especially engaging, detailing how each member of the U.S. Olympic team got started, how they have fared in competitions, and where they trained.

Speedskating.com www.speedskating.com ©

Ice, inline, or quad rolling—if it's serious skating, Speedskating.com covers it. Low on graphics but high on content, this site offers new headlines daily on all permutations of the sport as well as any media coverage received by the industry in general. Registering with the site allows a user to create a personal biography for the Skater Directory, post to message boards, and set up My Speed Page with information suited to specific interests.

Figure-Skating.com www.figure-skating.com

A site solely for the casual fan, Figure-Skating.com serves up biographical sketches of selected skaters and coaches, plus interactive games like Name that Quote, the weekly Fan Poll, or Mystery Skater, in which fans must identify a mystery skater from a blurry thumbnail photo. To find out what yesterday's favorite pros are doing now, check out the Where Are They Now link. Who would have guessed that the 1956 Olympic Gold medallist would be a renowned heart surgeon in the year 2001?

Soccernet www.soccernet.com

Although this ESPN-owned site touts the American word for the earth's favorite sport, don't be fooled. Soccernet is based out of London and is all about "football," in the rest of the world's sense of the word. The site features comprehensive, up-to-the-minute news and scores for England, Scotland, and Europe. Those searching for news on U.S. teams may be disappointed, though you can't help but be charmed by the writing style, as fresh and cheeky as would be expected from a bunch of English footie fanatics.

TSI Soccer www.tsisoccer.com

For anyone who plays soccer or simply must have a pair of striped calf socks, TSI's online store offers brand-name equipment like Mia Hamm T-shirts, Puma turf shoes, and Reebok warm-ups. The site is staffed by people who obviously love soccer, some of whom have played in the NCAA and the British Pub Leagues. What does that mean for you? Well-selected gear. Go to About Us for information on shipping, returns, and the like; there is no help page.

Fédération Internationale de Football Association
www.fifa.com ©

That's soccer to you, Yank. Dial up this page to discover (or revel in) the depths with which this sport is revered—every place but the United States, that is. FIFA features articles, interviews, regulations, laws of the game, lists of competitions, a calendar of events, and much, much more. There's also extensive coverage of the women's leg of this sport.

SoccerTimes.com www.soccertimes.com ©

A virtual who's who guide for soccer fans, SoccerTimes.com contains connections to all major MLS, U.S. National, NCAA, international, and youth teams. Though we might expect better design from this associate of ESPN.com, we were persuaded by the analysis and commentary found in the feature articles. Stick to the more newsy parts; some of the softer sections like Op/Ed offer content from two months ago.

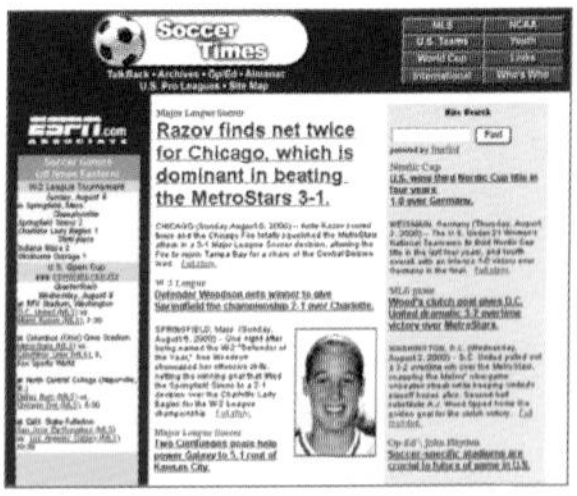

ZoomSoccer.com www.zoomsoccer.com

ZoomSoccer.com is that rare place where soccer fans can congregate without the risk of bloodshed. If the fear of getting crushed by the crowds has kept you away from important games, listen to them live on this site via RealAudio. Also check out ZoomSoccer TV, which offers fans' memories of their favorite teams on video, and Picturewire, a virtual album of classic plays captured on camera.

The Soccer Spot www.soccerspot.com

Forgoing the sport's characteristic frenzy, the internetsoccer.com network gives its American page a low-key tone and straight-up design. But just because The Soccer Spot minds its manners doesn't mean it's a stick in the virtual mud. The writing behind headlines like "Yes, Virginia, There Is an All-Star Game," is snappy and in-the-know, and does a good job adding flavor to the more ordinary schedules and scores. A solid source for followers of the MLS, USL, and national teams.

Juventus.com www.juventus.com

What do the players of the Juventus team do during the summer? Among other things, they answer questions submitted by visitors to their official site. The Juve Zone, the site's interactive portion, offers a form for sending comments to specific players, as well as photo albums and several 360-degree spinning tours of the Delle Alpi stadium. If you're looking for more serious fare—pre and post match analysis, team news, and RealVideo highlights—you'll find them at this site as well.

College Soccer Online www.collegesoccer.com

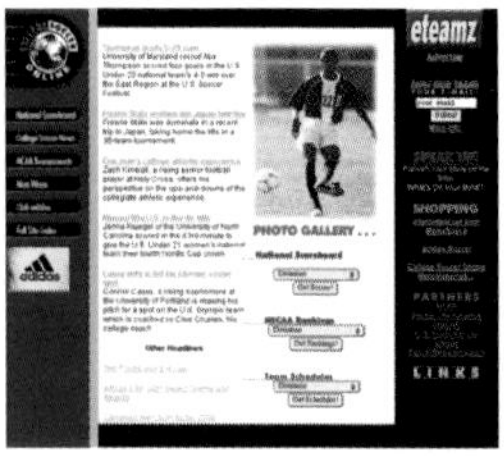

Colorful, laced with rollovers, and illustrated with random photos, College Soccer Online scores points for enthusiasm. Mixed into predictable information like news and NCAA tournament details are sections like Next Wave, which digs into off-season training tips and new trends in the sport (street play may soon win popularity). The only penalty we might award the site would be for inconsistent updating.

Football Unlimited www.footballunlimited.co.uk

Brought to you by the *London Guardian*, this is a comprehensive soccer site with stats, schedules, and eye-catching editorials. The site is meant to be more comprehensive than the newspaper, and is, with a simple format and quick-loading graphics. Beware the anglicized language and subject matter, but be sure to check out The Fiver: Football Unlimited's "tea-time take" on the world of football published every day at 5 p.m. EST.

Eurofinals365 www.eurofinals365.com

Though Eurofinals fans will have to wait until 2004 for the next games, surfing here will painlessly pass the time. New material is added daily on the events (past and future) and each of the 16 national teams that participated in the last ones. The Fun & Features section boasts a sillier side, with a place to choose a Miss Euro from among the top ten players' girlfriends and quotes gone wrong. To wit: "I heard the odds are 80-1 against us. Bet on Slovenia and you will earn a lot of money."

FC Bayern München www.fcbayern.de

Arguably the greatest German soccer team, FC Bayern grants its fans an eyeful of recent action on its site. The homepage lists headlines and links to a full photo gallery, while the Matches subpage goes into greater detail, describing past games and speculating on upcoming ones. Register for membership to win access to the site's newsletter and fan forums (as well as those on other Sportal Network sites, if you choose to share your info with them).

Soccer America www.socceramerica.com

Finally, after decades of European and South American popularity, soccer is on the rise in America. Not only are more kids playing the sport, but Major League Soccer has also become mainstream sporting entertainment. Follow MLS, international, or college soccer here; though low-frills, the site is passionate and up-to-date in its coverage of men's, women's, and youth teams. The site also offers Soccer Yellow Pages, invaluable for finding soccer-related organizations, clubs, businesses, and the like.

ManUtd.com www.manutd.com

It's nice to know that Internet technology has made it possible for the average netizen to see a panoramic view of the Manchester United Football Club's laundry room. But users who don't want to get quite that personal will also find this site a worthwhile source for player and manager profiles, news, and access to both radio and webcasts of the games. If you'd like to actually attend a game, see the Supporters section to tie up all of the ticketing and transportation details.

internetsoccer.com www.internetsoccer.com

Here's where the diehard fanatics are separated from the fair-weather

fans. Only true devotees will savor the site's exhaustive schedule of soccer games, info on international tournaments, and soccer news from Africa, Europe, Asia, and the Americas. The Live Scores section is updated every thirty seconds (which makes up for the skimpy Live Audio selection) and you can also get the news sent to your wireless device.

BigSoccer www.bigsoccer.com

According to BigSoccer, FIFA has more member nations than the United Nations. So it's not surprising that there are hundreds of rabid FIFA fans (not to mention followers of MLS and Olympic soccer) sounding off on this site's bulletin boards. More than 70 boards are constantly active, listed under subheadings for Brazil, Asia, Europe, North America, and Latin America. The site also offers a huge guide to soccer sites, though it's clear that the BBS's are where BigSoccer excels.

The Football Confederation www.footballconfederation.com

This site's eight-letter acronym stands for the Confederation of North, Central American, and Caribbean Association Football. One of the rare non-European soccer sites, this is less a fawning fan page than an informative news source. It posts new original articles on both men's and women's soccer in the Americas every five days, while updating the tournament commentary in its Signals subsection four times a month. The video library and newsletter are still under construction, so their links are currently empty.

BrasilFutebol.com www.brasilfutebol.com

Goooaaalll! Brazil is always a hot team internationally, and this site showcases it with short articles, live audio, and a big archive of photos from the games. Two features not to be missed: first, the Match Tracker, a window that ticks off the details of games in progress. Second, the Virtual Reality tour of the trophy room, which offers a rotating view until you zoom in on an award. Just beware the virtual nausea.

sporting goods

Teva www.teva.com

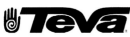

The inspiration for Tevas came to river guide Mark Thatcher back in 1982, when the soon-to-be-founder couldn't find a sandal suitable for navigating the Colorado River. The strappy shoe he invented may look delicate, but don't be fooled. Tevas can do battle with everything from cobblestones to hiking trails. The customer service page here is geared toward questions about the shoes rather than about the site; while we appreciate the information on cleaning and caring for Tevas, the site could stand some explanation of return policies and the like.

LiveToPlay.com www.livetoplay.com

If you need outdoor gear but don't want to pay outrageous prices, LiveToPlay.com is a good starting point. This jam-packed auction site lets you bid on everything from skateboards to camping stoves direct from well-known retailers like Jansport, Motorola, and Airwalk. Bidding for such desirable merchandise can be a sport unto itself; be prepared to meet some formidable competition!

Gear.com www.gear.com ©

Can't afford to join a gym? Well, that's no excuse to sit around the house: Gear.com has the equipment to keep you hale and hearty, all at closeout prices. More than 50 sports are represented here, including adventure travel, downhill skiing, and wakeboarding. Search by activity, brand, or for their newest items in stock. Gear.com will ship your purchases for a mere 25 cents an item, so go ahead and stock up.

Sneaker.com www.sneaker.com

Browse by sport for Nike, Adidas, Reebok, Puma, or Asics (among others), as well as shoes specially designed for tennis, golf, and soccer. The

selection isn't overwhelming, which makes for a manageable interface and easy surfing. You'll have 30 days to return merchandise, but be sure it's in the original packaging; else Sneaker.com may deny your refund.

Online Sports www.onlinesports.com ©

In addition to the basketball, soccer, and football gear you'd find at every other e-store, this site has equipment for sports you never knew existed, like broom hockey and corkball. Granted, the design isn't much to look at, but where else are you going to find a sparring body pad to practice your jeet kune do? Ideal for rugged individualists and eccentrics alike.

Fogdog Sports www.fogdog.com © ⓓ

Don't be misled by the URL; you won't find any chew toys here, just tons and tons of sporting equipment. Get all the gear and apparel for your favorite activity, from the majors (basketball, football, baseball, hockey) to the minors (lacrosse, gymnastics, wrestling). Browse the categories, sports, or concept shops, or just search by keyword. A wonderful alternative to shopping in chaotic, understaffed sporting goods stores.

lucy.com www.lucy.com ⓓ ⓞ

Here's the remedy for those with ill-fitting shorts and jog-bra envy. The Oregon-based e-tailer has found 900 different types of sports apparel to fit every body type, browsable by sport, keyword, or prefab stylish outfit. But Lucy doesn't just want to clothe you; the site's e-zine, Live and Learn, has a huge bank of motivational articles, nutrition advice, and inspirational stories from sporty women.

Nike.com www.nike.com ⓓ ⓞ ⓢ

Nike deserves props for beefing up its site with stunning visuals and loads of hand-crafted pages devoted to the world's top athletes, like CBN (the "Charles Barkley Network"). One click of the Store button will take you straight to hundreds of styles of the revered athletic shoes. Or, if you prefer a custom look, visit the new NIKE iD section and put together the perfect combo of base, trim, and midsole colors.

REI.com www.rei.com © ⓢ

The company that made it possible to look stylish while climbing a big hunk of granite has firmly established itself on the Net. After loading up on hiking, climbing, camping, cycling, and fishing gear at this massive store, be sure to pay a visit to the Learn and Share board, where you'll discover the best way to pack a backpack and the nicest places to hike around the world. There's even a gift registry here!

Capezio Dance Theatre Shop www.capeziorvc.com

Whether you're a prima ballerina or flamenco is your forte, Capezio Dance Theatre Shop has the dance and exercise gear to keep you on your toes. Get the leotards, unitards, jazz sneakers, and pointe shoes you need for rehearsals and performances. When your items arrive, test them gently—Capezio's return policy says no refunds on gear that looks broken in.

SportingAuction.com www.sportingauction.com

What makes SportingAuction.com cool enough to be included in this book? Well, for starters, a flat $5 shipping fee on any size order. That's right: whether you order a pair of rollerblades, a snowboard, a sleeping bag or all three, the site will ship the stuff right to your door for five bucks ($13 for oversized items). Everything sold here is brand-new and brand name, so if you're looking for a bargain, be sure to take a peek.

World Foot Locker Megastore Online www.footlocker.com

Jocks who can go 10 rounds with Tyson but refuse to brave the crowds at Foot Locker need not despair; they can now buy their favorite athletic shoes online. With more than 17,200 products and 260 brands, it's hard to conceive of a sneaker that isn't represented here—and endless inventory means terrific savings for you, sport-o. Need to return your shoe? Mail it in or take it to one of Foot Locker's 2,500 stores.

Patagonia Online Store www.patagonia.com

Browse by activity (backpacking, sailing, or ice climbing, for starters) to find jackets, pants, backpacks, outdoor accessories, and signature fleeces from Patagonia. All the gear here is top-quality and backed by a knowledgeable sales staff. The products are pricey ($155 for a fleece), but where else are you gonna go for a Gortex Ice-9 suit?

PlanetOutdoors.com www.planetoutdoors.com

For athletes who would rather look good than feel good, there's PlanetOutdoors.com. While it's true you can shop by sport, the site is also eager to help customers choose items from the more than 100 designer labels here, including Swiss Army and The North Face. Hey, you never know who you'll run into on that mountain top!

Pro Webwear.com www.prowebwear.com

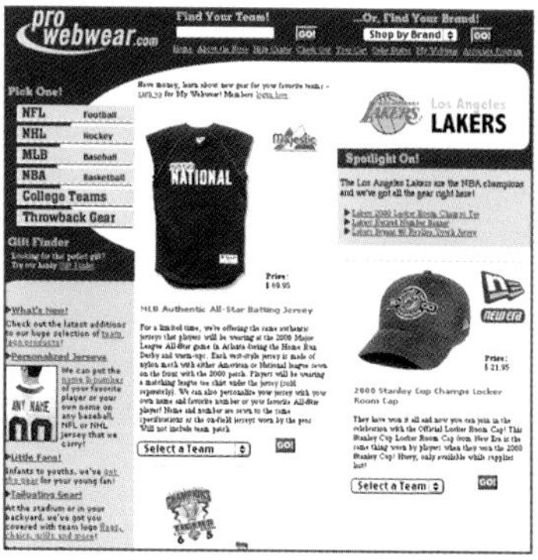

Wear your pride on your sleeve—literally—with a visit to Pro Webwear.com. Featuring hats, jerseys, and jackets emblazoned with the logos of college and professional teams, you'll finally be able to outfit yourself like those lunatics you see in sporting arenas all over the nation. For an extra-special treat, you can have your own name and your hero's number slapped on the NHL or NFL jersey of your choice.

ShopSports.com www.shopsports.com

An online sports superstore, this site has the fitness, outdoor, and athletic gear you love at prices that won't make you cramp up. All the big names are here, including Reebok, Adidas, and Wilson, but the limited space allowed in this review can hardly do justice to the exhaustive content at ShopSports.com. Before stocking your shopping cart, check out the weekly e-centives for worthwhile savings; shipping is free.

Sport Chalet www.sportchalet.com Ⓢ

You'd be hard pressed to find wider array of sporting goods online. Where else can you buy an inflatable kayak, a paintball gun, and a camping mess kit in one place? The thoughtful design makes it easy to browse—click on any item to get buyer's guides, a checklist of essentials, links to related products (especially safety gear), and tips on use along with the product's description.

Tailgate Town www.tailgatetown.com

How loyal a fan are you? Sure you tailgate, but do your true colors shine through on flags, coolers, chairs, and cups? Both college and professional teams are represented at Tailgate Town, so be sure to stock up on supplies, lest the other guys out-spirit you. If the hats and jerseys don't draw you, the keg-shaped grill just might.

MVP.com **www.mvp.com** © Ⓢ

Looking to buy a football but don't know your polyurethane from your polyvinyl chloride? Get the skinny on pigskin (and any other sporting equipment) directly from the pros that know: Elway, Jordan, and Gretzky. The powerhouse players have teamed up to bring you one of the most info-packed sporting goods sites online. Check out the buyer's guides here for expert advice on choosing equipment and protective gear; with advice from these guys, how could you possibly go wrong?

GearGoddess www.geargoddess.com

This site's information on gear for female athletes comes from women whose frustration with gear shopping drove them to do some serious research. Guides here cover cycling, snow sports, outdoors, and running, offering both buying tips and a gear-finder that seeks out products based on price, brand, and skill level. The only thing the site doesn't offer is a way to buy the goods directly.

Fila www.fila.com

Sporting goods companies always have the most inspirational television commercials—your favorite athletes soaring through the air, showing off only the best moves. Fila may not make you move like them, but they'll sure help you look like them. Athletes will appreciate the ease with which you can find activity-specific gear (from soccer cleats to training pants and T-shirts) organized by both sport and gender. Product descriptions are sometimes lacking, but detailed pictures help you make the final call.

dsports.com www.dsports.com © Ⓢ

An 18-year-old boy named Dick Stack, $300 from his nana's cookie jar, and a dream—these were the seeds from whence sprouted Dick's Sporting Goods. Fifty years and 85 stores later, the company has developed dsports.com to sell its crazy range of products to online athletes. Everything from backpacks to hockey pucks comes with a buying guide to help you pick the right one, and a toll-free service number is available for further assistance.

JustBalls.com www.justballs.com ©

In this world of superstores and warehouses, it's nice to find a place devoted to a single type of product. JustBalls.com carries literally every type of ball, from medicine to pingpong to Nerf. Once you've got the balls, read the online encyclopedia and rules database, which provides rules and strategies for a variety of games.

Champs Sports www.champssports.com

A source for sporting equipment, clothing, shoes, and accessories that's backed by 650 brick-and-mortar stores means you'll never have to worry about where to return items. But considering the brand names sold here—including Puma, Wilson, Rawlings, and Nike—you'll likely want to hold on to any purchases. The stock contains a boggling 17,000 different items, which is sorted by sport, brand, or bargain price to make it manageable.

The Athlete's Foot www.theathletesfoot.com

The Athlete's Foot claims to be the only retailer with a research and development center to evaluate major athletic shoe brands for durability, construction, and comfort. Visitors to the company's site can read up on its findings and then flip right over to the e-commerce end to shop for shoes and apparel. The selection is truly enormous—our search for a pair of New Balance sneaks returned 180 different products—so refine your search as much as possible by entering a brand, gender, or activity.

Athleta.com www.athleta.com

For years, female athletes have struggled with athletic gear designed by and for men. Enter Athleta.com, a site that provides products and advice specifically made for active women. Each product is hand-selected and fully reviewed by Athleta's team of self-confessed runners, cyclists, surfers, and gym rats. You'll find clothes for everything from bouldering to in-line skating and yoga, but it's not cheap: a sleek tank top goes for $35-$55.

tennis

Tennis.com www.tennis.com

Whether you like to serve-and-volley, bash from the baseline, or just watch, this tennis info hub provides pro tennis news, gear shopping guidance, match listings, and an informative instruction section with tips for improving your game. The site is super-accessible and geared to fans (not fanatics) who like to play the game; the content is solid, if predictable, with a couple of pleasant surprises, like the Sport Science section.

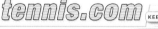

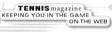

TennisOnline www.tennisonline.com ©

For people who realize that there are more people playing this sport than just the ones flattening the grass at Wimbledon, TennisOnline is the Web site to check out. In addition to pro news, the site offers rankings, results, and a who's who for college and amateur teams. On the most grassroots level, it discusses what can be done to promote the sport and allows players to organize a Web page with schedules and rankings for their own competitive teams.

MensTennis.com www.menstennis.com

Game, set, match. In addition to daily news features to keep fans up to date on the latest matches, MensTennis.com offers exclusive interviews with players, health tips, tennis instruction, television broadcast schedules, and background information to help bring anyone up to speed. Handy links help direct fans to more specialized locales, including an online pro shop with comprehensive buying guides.

Tennis Company www.tenniscompany.com

Not sure where to find that Hyper Hammer 3.3? This site offers online shopping for a ton of racquets (including that one), balls, shoes, grips, and bags, and if you buy a set of strings along with a racquet, the certified staff will install them for free. Other helpful additions include product review articles that rate the pros and cons of similar brands, a racquet buying guide, and a small stock of used racquets. In fact, the only thing we found missing here is a privacy policy.

TennisONE www.tennisone.com ©

This is the site that can teach you the Sampras serve. It offers extensive lessons using photographs and text, as well as audio tips and videos of the pros performing textbook strokes. It also has up to date news on the professional and senior tennis circuits, as well as journal entries from the site's correspondents. To play like the pros, you'll also need professional-quality equipment—read the research here on which gear performs the best.

TennisMatch www.tmatch.com

TennisMatch may incorporate a few too many pictures of Anna Kournikova into its site design, but it doesn't neglect other tennis stars. Both the magazine and the e-zine that bear its name provide well-rounded updates and features on the sport's professionals. Check the Buzz section for interesting tidbits (e.g. "2 new juniors bloom at the Easter Bowl") or Services for cool instructional QuickTime videos, but skip the unsecured online shopping page.

Australian Open www.ausopen.org © ⓞ

Tennis is Australia's most attended sport, but even tennis fans living outside the Outback will appreciate the courtside view of the country's grand slam tournament that its Web site affords. Cameras located around the court feed still pictures to the site, while tickers on the homepage track the players' progress. When the tourney is over, the site offers articles and speculation on the coming year, and archives of video and photography.

US Open www.usopen.org © ⓞ

This site covers America's only chance in pro tennis for a home court advantage, offering real-time scores, live cameras, and up-to-date news while the event is happening. The rest of the year, check here for ticket information, as well as articles discussing the history of the tournament and some of its greatest champions. In the few instances where it lacks coverage, it will refer you to the USTA site for more information.

ATP Tour www.atptour.org

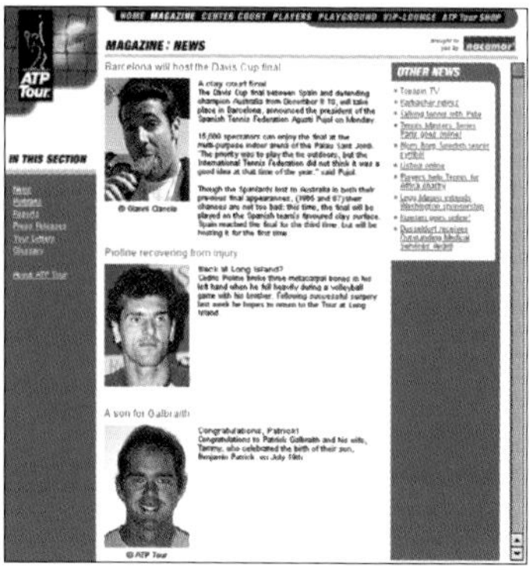

All of the major men's professional tournaments fall under the umbrella of the ATP, so the organization's official site is the destination of choice for broad coverage of them. It affords users the opportunity to chat with stars like Agassi, watch live coverage of selected events, and read an online version of the ATP's magazine. The site is also an excellent reference for games past, with 200 video clips and an archive of articles that goes back to 1990.

The Wimbledon Championships www.wimbledon.com ©

The oldest tennis tourney and some of the newest sports coverage technology add up to one dazzling Web site. During the tournament, top-notch features include live cameras you can aim from your PC, a downloadable scoreboard with live pictures, and real-time radio broadcasts. Articles discuss each player's chances as well as important issues in tennis. During the rest of the year, some of the best moments in Wimbledon history are accessible on video.

Davis Cup www.daviscup.org ⓓ

The Davis Cup, the only tennis tournament in which players compete on teams for their countries, is skillfully monitored by this sleekly designed site. The day's news fills a scroll bar on the right side of the page, while elegant rollover menus on the left offer access to results, teams, Davis Cup history, and panoramic views of the venues where the games are held each year. During the tournament, scores are updated several times per minute and live audio coverage is available.

Official Site of Roland Garros www.frenchopen.org ©

You don't have to live in France to love the French Open, and when players head to the clay courts of Roland Garros, you can just head for this site. Its in-depth coverage of the tournament includes live cameras, scoreboards, and essential information like downloadable driving directions for your WAP device. Users can take an interactive tour of the facilities, which shows where all of those cameras are located. However, like many tournament sites, this one is simply an archive off-season.

water sports

Yachtingnet www.yachtingnet.com

Landlubbers beware! If you don't know what a davit system is, Yachtingnet is not for you. This community hub caters solely to the power and sail boating community, with an emphasis on luxury boats and a depth that only a sailor could love. Read about the newest yacht to hit the water, use the Boat Finder to hone in on your dream boat, or peruse the articles on sailing destinations. If the jargon trips you up, someone in the hefty forums can probably help.

Americas Cup www.americascup.org

The Quokka Sports network brings its immersive approach to sports coverage to one of the sailing world's biggest events, pairing news and standings with high-tech tools like broadband race footage, virtual sloop tours, and the Performance Viewer, an interactive graph that lets you compare how different teams fare under variables like seasonal weather and wind. Of course, coverage is at its best during the race, but there's plenty to keep a fan occupied even after the cup has been won.

Skin Diver Online www.skin-diver.com

If you don't yet dream of rubbing fins with a four-eyed butterfish, you soon will. Skin Diver Online amazes with breathtaking underwater photography of tropical locales like the Cayman Islands; it also gives the info you'll need to get there. The site also covers diving's practical details, with a how-to guide for beginning divers, underwater photography tips, and gear comparisons.

Scuba Diving www.scubadiving.com

Though design seems to have been lost in the translation from print to pixel, all the information from *Scuba Diving* magazine appears to have come through unscathed. Dig around to find gems like eight ways to dodge decompression sickness, the 100 best diving destinations, or what to do when jellyfish attack. The gear guide is superior to many we've seen—click on any part of the diver in the illustration to get great advice on that piece of equipment.

Speedo www.speedo.com
Don't worry: not all of Speedo's swimsuits are of the grape-smuggling variety. In fact, most of the gear seems to be designed for folks who don't confine their water activity to lounging around the pool. In addition to racing suits, there's also stuff like snorkel sets, swim stroke monitors, bathing caps, and radio watches. The prices are a little steep, but keep in mind that these products are made to last.

ScubaSource.com www.scubasource.com ©

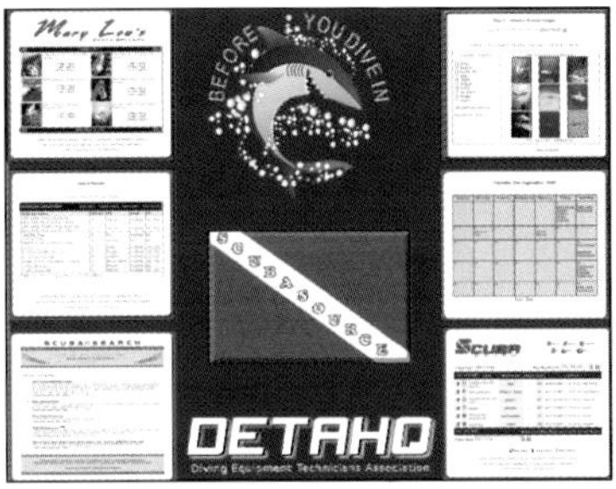

The number one piece of advice from Dive Master King Neptune on the ScubaSource.com's scuba board is to keep a controlled rate of breathing—even when the mermaids show up. Of course, there is also more serious information to be had on this extremely comprehensive hub, with separate sections devoted to the who, where, and how of the sport. Women will appreciate the several pages written especially for them, and everyone will value having access to such active community bulletin boards.

RowersWorld.com www.rowersworld.com
Think of it as your go-to for all your rowing needs. Though original editorial content is lacking, you'll find extensive offerings including discussion boards, photo archives, rowing gear, and racing updates for national and international teams at the junior, collegiate, and elite levels. Check out the slide show for some inspirational rowing photography or head over to the site's classifieds for deals on ergometers or the latest jobs for rowing professionals.

Outdoorplay.com www.outdoorplay.com
An e-tailer devoted entirely to kayaking, rafting, and canoeing. This site sells boats, apparel, outfitting, and instructional books and videos, each with a clear description and picture, but even if you're not shopping, you'll appreciate the informative tone. Among the contents are essential tips like how to make a wet exit (bail out of an overturned kayak) and videos that let you see various rivers through the eyes of rafters.

Overtons.com www.overtons.com © Ⓢ
Yes, it's got the bathing suits and water wings you'll find at every other sporting goods site, but where else are you going to find doggie life preservers, boat engine parts, and barefoot water-skiing gear? Overtons.com can even deliver a boat to your home. Ahoy, me hearties!

United States Sailing Association www.ussailing.org

When the flood of information on this site's homepage threatens to drown you, hold on to that little menu in the upper left. It uses rollovers to break the mammoth contents into simple categories like Youth Sailing, Racing, Olympic Sailing, and Education and Access, which each further break down into subcategories like Getting Started and Safety at Sea. If you're brave enough to tackle the homepage, you'll also get news and regatta results.

U.S. Diving www.usadiving.org

No belly-floppers here. U.S. Diving is devoted to the art of synchronized diving, where divers perform similar jumps off of either the three or 10-meter platform. Competitive divers can read the latest diving news, get schedules and standings for the national swim teams, brush up on regulations, find a meet or club in their area, or check out the history section to learn about the early days of the sport.

Boating.com www.boating.com

Who better for a beginning boater to talk to than a salty dog who has already mastered the tricks of smooth sailing? Boating.com packs its simple site with a myriad of discussion forums where weekend enthusiasts can swap advice and anecdotes on sailing, maintenance, fishing, and more. The homepage also offers news and nautical event listings, while the hefty Resources section has handy tools like tide predictors, surf cams, and weather reports.

swimmersworld.com www.swimmersworld.com ©

Chock full of news and resources, swimmersworld.com is a great place to find a coach or tutor, fetch news on your favorite Olympic stars, or research future meets and clubs for the family. Use the swimming search engine to find college and club pages among its 2,500 links, or visit the discussion pages to hook up with fellow swimmers. Avid swimmers will love interactive tools like the taper calculator, which helps you calculate your potential for the year with pre- and post-shave stats.

SailNet www.sailnet.com © ⓓ

A must-surf for novice sailors who can't tell their boom from their backstay, SailNet has a huge, animated Learn to Sail section that uses graphs, rollovers, and boat diagrams to familiarize beginners with their craft and the rules of the water. More advanced sailing is also addressed, with extensive sections on buying a boat, renovating it inside and out, racing, and joining the boating community. A superlative resource.

Canoe & Kayak www.canoekayak.com

If you're a longtime subscriber to *Canoe & Kayak*, you may want to pass this site by. However, if you haven't caught every article since 1998, you'll find many of them peppered throughout the magazine's site. Sections detail where to go in your boat, what to take, and how to go about it—"Kids and Canoe Camping" and "Source to Sea Trek in Maine" were two recent pieces. You'll also find a mid-sized bank of links to resources like outfitters, guides, and paddling schools.

weekend diversions

volleyball.com www.volleyball.com ⓓ

In 1895, a YMCA instructor in Massachusetts set out to create a game that blended elements of basketball, baseball, tennis, and handball but demanded less physical contact. You guessed volleyball, right? Find out more about the sport's origins and buy gear for the game at volleyball.com. Intermediate and competitive players will find tournament listings and plenty of shopping on these pages, but the discussion boards are quiet, indeed.

Streetplay.com www.streetplay.com © ⓞ

Revisit the asphalt playgrounds of your youth on Streetplay.com. While the site is geared to baby boomers, it will spark nostalgia for anyone who played stickball, stoopball, marbles, or hopscotch as a kid. The emphasis is squarely on urban play (especially summers in the Big Apple), with stories and pictures of favorite childhood moments and an encyclopedia that explains the rules of games like 'Asses Up'.

Ultilinks www.ultilinks.com ©

This site's modest name overlooks the fact that it offers much more than simply links for the ultimate frisbee enthusiast. Original interviews with players, tournament results, and rules (in multiple languages) are just a few of the things found within the clean interface. The Learn section holds two new articles each month, one for beginners and one for more advanced players, and naturally, a huge selection of links is available for further instruction.

Croquet World Online Magazine www.croquetworld.com

San Francisco croquet enthusiasts created this site to celebrate their favorite sport however and wherever it is played. They cover matches and gather results from lawns across the world. The Game section teaches basics and finer points, as well as answering pressing questions on game form like "How 'wristy' is your swing?"

Into The Wind www.intothewind.com

While you may not exactly be panting for instructions on what type of kite to use when sea kayaking, the folks at Into The Wind also provide friendly kite shopping and a big selection of beginner models, including hundreds of traditional and stunt kites, kits, and supplies. See Kite 101 for the how-to angle, excerpted from the Pocket Guide to Kite Flying (a full version of the book comes free with each order).

winter sports

Board the World www.boardtheworld.com © ⓓ

You don't have to be a master of the Frontside 360 Roast Beef Grab to enjoy the deluge of snowboarding information at Board the World. Besides daily updates on snow conditions in multiple countries, the site has resort reviews, an e-zine, links to gear shopping, and advice for novices and advanced boarders alike. The Air 101 section is a must-surf for shredders looking to round out their repertoire of tricks—it holds instructions and photos for a number of death-defying feats.

KindSnow.com www.kindsnow.com ⓓ

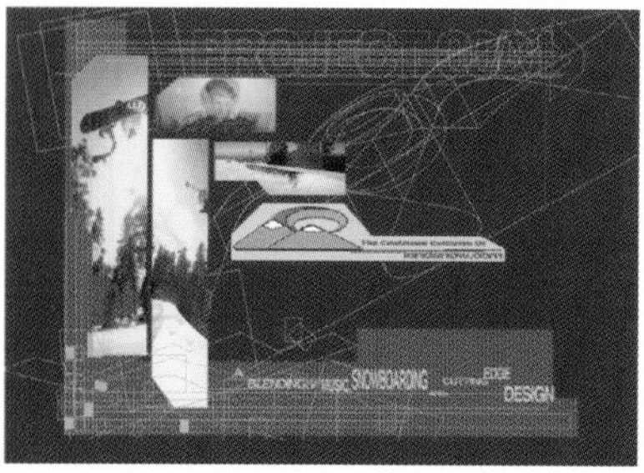

While snowboarders are grinding their teeth and waiting for the barren, snowless days of summer to pass, the guys behind Kind-Snow are redesigning their site in preparation for the season. Each year brings a new, slick version of the e-zine with improved features—this year's includes an expanded terrain park section and multimedia trick tips. Get the Flash plug-in to fully enjoy the show.

MountainZone.com www.mountainzone.com ©

Master those snowy slopes or just look really cool at the lodge. MountainZone.com has an even mix of information and gear shopping, with sections for skiing, boarding, mountain biking, hiking, and climbing. New how-tos, sports-celebrity profiles, and terrifying expedition tales are posted every few days. For those who are bashful of the bunny slopes, the narrated multimedia videos will take you as close to the scenery as is possible without a lift ticket.

SkiNet.com www.skinet.com ©

Before you rack your skis and head to the mountains, log on to SkiNet.com, designed by the experts at *Ski, Skiing,* and *Freeze* magazines. Though the site is a bit heavy on product promotions, there's an avalanche of ski-related data here, from daily snowfall updates on major mountains to gear reviews and quirky editorials like "How Rude are the Slopes?"

SkiReview.com www.skireview.com

Lust over all the rippingest ski gear this season at SkiReview.com, a consumer-driven site with the skinny on skis, poles, boots, and goggles. While product reviews are the site's supposed forte, the pickings are unfortunately slim—a click on the women's skis section got us just one review per model in most cases. Slope and road conditions, a gear market-place, and Ski Talk are some of the other options. See Skiing 101 for an exhaustive collection of instructions and tips for all styles and skill levels.

GoSki www.goski.com ©

When your usual ski spot starts to get old, check GoSki for recommended ski resorts as far a field as Sweden, Andorra, and India. Contact information and user reviews are listed for each resort, along with standard ski info like the national weather forecast and reports on the latest snow gear. Any site that urges, "Quit the Day Job, Call in Sick" is definitely onto something!

Snowlink www.snowlink.com

That Snowlink offers a complete guide to snowshoeing should tell you just how vigilant the site is about addressing every possible facet of winter resort sports. Some of the articles you'll encounter are original to the site, while other material originated elsewhere (there are, after all, 800 different links here). If that seems overwhelming, start at the Tips & Pics section—it has basics like how to avoid frostbite, as well as helpful explanations of site features.

Ski Racing Magazine www.skiracing.com

A look into racing life crafted by writers and editors who know their slopes. This slick sister-site to the print magazine by the same name has stories on all sorts of skiing, from alpine to nordic, freestyle to snowboarding. The profiles section boasts interviews with such famous ski-racing personalities as Olympic darling Picabo Street, who crashed and burned in Switzerland in 1998; click on Features for the latest from the Olympic teams.

SkiCentral www.skicentral.com ⓞ

A cool search engine that only returns ski and snow sport related results, SkiCentral is the tool to use to track down weather reports, local clinics, gear auctions, and more. When you enter a term, the site's automated search bot, SkiWiz, will actually try to anticipate what you're looking for and offer suggestions for how to refine your search. New sites are added daily—you'll find a list of the top 100 behind the New Sites link.

SkiTown.com www.skitown.com ⓓ

Calling all ski bums! The resort finder here can help you find bigger and better slopes at resorts across the U.S. and Canada. The site sorts lodging by geographical area, activities, terrain, services (like day care), and a host of other criteria. While it's clearly a commercial venture to promote SkiTown.com's resort network, there are hundreds of viable vacation spots listed here.

United States Ski Team www.usskiteam.com

Witness Michael Michaelchuck's record-breaking halfpipe spins or Hannu Manninen's spectacular snow dive—the news on the United States Ski Team's site comes with super clear RealPlayer videos that download quickly to bring all the mogul mastery of competitive skiing to your computer. Click on the fasTV.com video player to see what highlights are available for viewing.

Dogsled.com www.dogsled.com ©

All the adventure, none of the frostbite. When the Iditarod Sled Dog Race begins in Anchorage during the first weekend in March, this site features video interviews with the mushers and Radio Iditarod, audio feed that takes listeners from checkpoint to checkpoint. Dogsled.com also includes photos of the race, biographies of the participants, a kids' area, and (for the off season) a Reference Desk with Iditarod history, race rules, and a trail map.

SnowboarderReview.com www.snowboarderreview.com © ⓓ

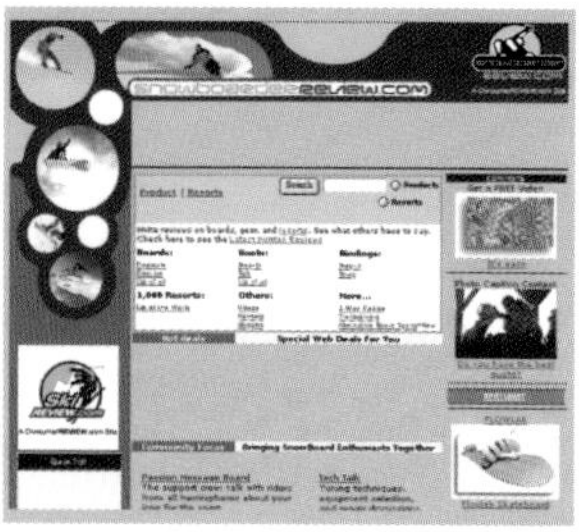

The best way we've found to compare boards and bindings (short of trying them all yourself) are the consumer reviews at SnowboarderReview.com. Get the cyber-skinny on which boots cause blisters and which boards rock, plus vital views on resorts and land boards. You're a novice? The Snow Boarding 101 link tells what gear you need to stay warm.

wrestling

Amateur Wrestler www.amateurwrestler.com

No slick, WWF theatrics here—Amateur Wrestler covers the world of "real wrestling" with an emphasis on NCAA and Olympic action. The articles in the Training and Health sections, therefore, address serious issues like rapid weight loss and the benefits of summer training, and are infused with insights that the writers accrued as competetive wrestlers. The forums are equally enlightening, and include a much-needed women's wrestling board among the discussions of high school wrestling and coaching.

WWF.com www.wwf.com

The World Wrestling Federation is back with more force than a power-slam by all three hundred pounds of Cactus Jack. The newly sleek WWF Web site serves as a companion to the televised action, providing bios of all the Superstars and Divas and results of recent face-offs. Though you can't watch any matches online (unless you pay per view), the Web-casts section archives past footage and Byte This interviews.

Wrestle Arena www.wrestlearena.com © ⓓ

Quick, who's the best wrestler of all time: Stone Cold Steve Austin or Macho Man? Compelling arguments for both are posted in the forum on the Interactive portion of Wrestle Arena. Other sections on the site recap recently televised and pay-per-view WCW, ECW, and WWF matches, detail fictitious news (all stories in The World are fabricated), and offer up different columnists' perspectives. You won't find any video in the Multimedia section, but rather clips from wrestlers' theme songs and audio interviews from the live radio show, *The Edge*.

The NukeSylo Network www.nukesylo.com © ⓞ

The pioneer of play-by-play chats and pay-per-view wrestling matches has improved on the now common idea by adding IRC software with voice chat capabilities. By downloading NukeSylo Network's software, you can speak to other wrestling fans through a microphone attached to your computer, or bat instant messages back and forth. Conversation fodder comes in the form of news briefs and stats, and totally crass locker room banter on the Rage board.

WrestleLine www.wrestleline.com

Did you know that there are also thriving pro wrestling communities in the U.K., Japan, and beyond? SportsLine's predictably comprehensive wrestling site offers blow-by-choreographed-blow accounts of recent matches internationally. For longer commentary, skip the WOW magazine (not updated since 1999) and head to the columns for nine well-spoken viewpoints.

youth sports

SIKids.com www.sikids.com

For any Little Leaguer who's ever wanted to draft his own major league team, *Sports Illustrated*'s kid site comes through. The Bat-o-Matic gives kids four million virtual dollars to draft a team, and scores it according to real stats. SIKids.com also has advice, sports news, and video clips of cool plays, making this site a quality junior version of the grown-up magazine. Be sure to click on Toons for fun animated shorts.

Kids Sports Network www.ksnusa.org

Just how well trained is the coach of your kid's basketball team? The San Antonio-based Kids Sports Network is an organization that's dedicated to great youth coaching. The site posts articles on youth sports issues and outlines coaching standards that include keeping mental and physical abuse off the playing field. Community sports programs like Operation Night Hoops and the Basketball Jamboree are also profiled here.

KIDS Sports Network

Black Belt for Kids www.blackbeltmag.com/bbkids

A far cry from the Hollywood touch of the *Karate Kid*, this surprisingly sophisticated site makes an impact with the variety of information it contains. There is advice on improving skills, but also poetry expressing love for the art, interviews with top martial art experts, and no-holds-barred debunking of the moves in karate flicks. Kids will actually like the When I Was Your Age section's advice from karate pros, and can email a question to be answered in the "Ask the Masters" column.

KidsHealth www.kidshealth.org

Sponsored by the Nemours Foundation, KidsHealth earns its stripes by providing extensive news and advice for children's physical and emotional health, written in three distinct age-appropriate tones for use by kids, adults, and teens. Parents can turn here to find out more about their child's infection, nutrition, and other health issues; kids find articles like "Dealing with feelings" and "My body," and teens can get answers to questions about growing up that they're too embarrassed to ask elsewhere.

InfoSports www.infosports.net

So you've reluctantly volunteered to officiate your child's Little League season and suddenly realize you need help. InfoSports is a good place to go when seeking advice from parents and coaches on the rules of the game. The site's forums cover smaller youth sports like cheerleading, swimming, and softball, as well as the bigger ones (basketball, baseball, and the like). Some teams also use the site to find people to play with, and locate tournaments and games.

SchoolSports.com www.schoolsports.com

Not much can be said for media coverage of high school sports—except on the local level. But fortunately, SchoolSports.com has stepped up to the plate with this site for high school athletes, coaches, and fans. Catch the highlights from games around the country, see who'll be the hottest recruits for college teams, and get tips on boosting team spirit in the Coaches' Corner. Game schedules are updated daily.

VarsityOnline.com www.varsityonline.com

This site's coverage of varsity high school sports may rely heavily on the contributions of teen reporters, but don't expect it to read like the back pages of a high school paper. The news on schools across the nation is clear-cut, thorough, and supplemented by daily scores, rosters, and photographs. Currently, the site's network only extends to a dozen states; click on the national map to see if and when it will include yours.

The Female Athlete.com www.thefemaleathlete.com
Mixed in amongst the ponytail batting helmets, beaded "sports" chokers, and *Cosmo Girl* tone is some solid information for athletic women. The Just for Girls section profiles exceptional athletes and features articles about the sports experience written by high schoolers, touching on some very important topics like eating disorders and discouragement. Conversely, the Parents & Coaches section offers insight into how to be a solid mentor. Note: reading some of the articles requires entering a lot of unnecessary personal information.

Kid-e-sport www.kid-e-sport.com ©

Learn how to prevent your kids from dropping out of field hockey, or how to deal with the obnoxious coach who inspired the move—Kid-e-sport may seem like a children's site with its fun, colorful design but it's an invaluable resource for sporting parents. Peruse stories on every sport from archery to in-line skating and soccer, or read up on mental health and self-esteem for jocks. An abundance of research, fabulous navigation, and online shopping make this a must-see for any parent.

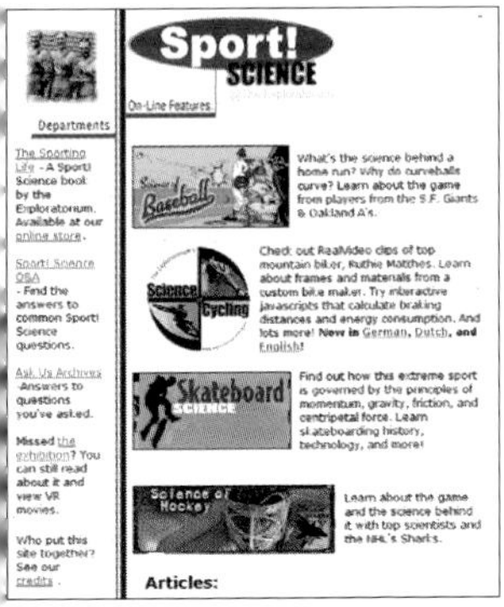

Sport! Science@The Exploratorium
www.exploratorium.edu/sports
What makes a basketball bounce and a curveball curve? This subsite of the famed science museum merges the spirit of Einstein and the magic of Michael Jordan to explore the fun side of sports physics. Clever articles and RealVideo clips address principles like momentum and gravity in an engaging format that wee athletes will love. There are also activities kids can do at home while reading along, though the multimedia experiments are by far the best.

SportsHuddle.com www.sportshuddle.com
College-bound stars, perennial bench-warmers, and the obsessed parents of both will appreciate having a resource like SportsHuddle.com. The site helps eliminate the confusion surrounding college recruitment, while providing techniques and health tips to assure that a student athlete will be a hot prospect. Specific pages for individual schools and teams are also available through the site, as is access to local newspaper coverage of varsity sports (though only for a handful of teams).

Kids' Zone www.cbs.sportsline.com/u/kids
Sports buffs of all ages can visit CBS SportsLine's Kids' Zone (but those under 15 will like it the most). The site divides its coverage between NHL, NBA, NFL, and Major League Baseball, with rapidly updated photos and game summaries tailored to fit an early teen attention span. But don't let little Mighty Ducks stray into the Stuff link unless you want them to buy a toy zamboni—it's just a shopping section.

glossary

bandwidth
Refers to the size of the data pipeline. To have higher bandwidth is to have a faster Internet connection that carries more information.

broadband
Refers to a high-speed Internet connection such as T-1 or DSL.

bulletin board system (bbs)
A message database where people can log in and leave broadcast messages for others, usually grouped into topics.

cache
Pronounced "cash," this refers to a temporary place to store files. Your browser's cache holds Web pages you've recently visited so it can load them again quickly when you return.

commissioner
In fantasy sports, the person responsible for managing the draft, overseeing trades, and tracking stats and scores.

cookie
A file put on your computer by a Web site so that it can "recognize" you at a later time. Though often used to target advertising, cookies also record passwords and enable online shopping carts.

cybercitizen
A citizen of the Internet, or a member of the cybercommunity. Also known as a netizen.

e-newsletter
An electronic newsletter delivered by email on a daily, weekly, or monthly basis. Many sites offer e-newsletters as a way for fans to keep up-to-date without having to revisit the site.

e-zine
The upstart Web counterpart of print magazines. Thousands of e-zines dot the cyber landscape, offering a veritable feast of info on every topic from news and opinion to sex and snowboarding.

e-commerce
(electronic commerce) is the buying and selling of goods on the Internet. Also called e-business or e-tailing (electronic retailing).

fantasy sports
A pastime where sports enthusiasts manage fictitious teams made up of professional players. The teams are scored according to the real-life performance of their players.

faq
A frequently asked question, or a list of frequently asked questions posted on a newsgroup or Web site.

firewall
A computer system that functions like a security guard to make sure that certain types of information can't enter or leave a private network. Many large corporations have firewalls.

flaming
Posting an obnoxious message on a public newsgroup, in a chat room, or in email. (*see also, netiquette*)

flash
Software program used to create animated graphics on a Web site. If a site has a glitzy introduction on its splash page, you can bet that Flash was used to create it.

gamecast
Any live recreation of game action that includes diagrams, scoreboards, or illustrations.

handheld device
Any type of computer that's smaller than a laptop, like a Palm Pilot, Windows CE, or WAP-enabled phone. (*see also, pda and wap*)

head-to-head games
A relatively new type of fantasy sports game that pits two teams in a league against each other each week. Head-to-head games take place in addition to regular league play.

netiquette
Etiquette on the Internet. Spamming or flaming your friends on the Web are examples of bad netiquette.

newbie
A Web freshman—new to the Internet and obviously so.

pda
Acronym for personal digital assistant, those handheld organizers—like the Palm Pilot—that inspire in some users the other type of PDA (public display of affection).

plug-in
An application that works in conjunction with your browser. Examples are RealAudio, which lets you listen to streaming music on the Internet, and Shockwave, which lets you view animations and games.

portal
A large hub site such as Yahoo! that offers a multitude of services, usually including news headlines, a search engine, feature content, and online tools.

real-time
Live. For example, real-time scores are scores that are updated as they change.

rollover
Graphic or text on a Web page that is activated when the cursor moves (or "rolls") over it.

rotisserie baseball
The original term for what is now called fantasy sports, the pastime born at New York's La Rotisserie Francaise restaurant.

shockwave
Software used to create many of the interactive games and animations on the Web. Visit www.shockwave.com to see the program strut its stuff.

simulcast
A text chat that is scheduled around a real world event. For example, fans of *The Simpsons* might log on to a simulcast during the show to exchange comments as they watch.

spam
Unsolicited junk email. Your email provider may offer spam-blocking, which filters out these annoying messages.

splash page
A lead-in page to a Web site (often animated) that appears on screen for just a few seconds.

streaming
When data is transferred in a steady and continuous stream. Listen to an Internet radio station, for example, and you're listening to music that is being streamed to your computer.

triplecast
Simultaneous broadcasts of a program over television, radio, and the Internet.

wap
(wireless application protocol) A format that allows users to view wireless Internet sites on certain handheld devices like cell phones and Palm Pilots. Such devices are referred to as WAP-enabled.

webcam
A video camera, usually attached directly to a computer, which feeds its footage to a Web site. A live cam is one that shows live streaming video.

webcast
A video program (often live) that is broadcast over the Web.

index